PRAYER
Your Foundation for Success

KENNETH COPELAND

KCP
PUBLICATIONS

KCP Publications
Fort Worth, Texas

Prayer — Your Foundation for Success

ISBN 0-88114-273-5   #30-0019

Unless otherwise indicated, all Scripture quotations are from the KING JAMES VERSION.

Published by KCP Publications
Fort Worth, Texas 76192

Cover Illustration - David A. Day

Contents

Contents

A Message from Kenneth Copeland

Early in my ministry, I learned a vital lesson: For any effort to be successful, it must be backed by prayer. Effective praying is the key to success in *every* area of life.

Your aim in prayer is to be effective. Jesus is the perfect example of One who knows how to pray and get results. Jesus spent hours separated from the people, praying and fellowshipping with His heavenly Father. The time He spent in prayer prepared Him to minister effectively.

As a believer, you can achieve the same results that Jesus did during His earthly ministry—and more. Jesus said, *He that believeth on me, the works that I do shall he do also; and greater works than these shall he do; because I go unto my Father* (John 14:12). These "greater works" can be accomplished today, but only by believers who have a deep, sincere prayer life with God.

This book is designed to strengthen your relationship with God through an awareness of the importance of prayer. With a solid foundation from the Word of God, you will understand the basic principles of prayer: its purpose, how to pray and how to get results.

As you read and study *Prayer—Your Foundation for Success*, I pray for you according to Ephesians 1:17,18 that you have the spirit of wisdom and revelation in the knowledge of God and that the eyes of your understanding will be enlightened to know the truth.

Kenneth Copeland

Chapter I
Prayer Secrets

Prayer is the foundation of every successful Christian endeavor. Time spent with God is vital if you desire a fruitful Christian life. As the foundation of *every* Christian endeavor it plays a vital role in living a successful Christian life. Study the lives of the great men and women of God from the past, and you will see the strong emphasis they placed on prayer. Without prayer, they would never have been able to achieve such tremendous results.

Throughout the New Testament we can see the value of prayer in the founding of the early churches. The Apostle Paul prayed and interceded many hours for the new believers. In Ephesians 1:16 he wrote: *I cease not to give thanks for you, making mention of you in my prayers.* In Colossians 1:3 he said: *We give thanks to God and the Father of our Lord Jesus Christ, praying always for you.* In 1 Thessalonians 5:17 he instructed the church to *pray without ceasing.* Luke 18:1 says, *Men ought always to pray and not to faint.*

It is not enough to know that we should pray. We need to know *why.* Look at Ephesians 4:14-16:

That we henceforth be no more children, tossed to and fro, and carried about with every wind of doctrine,by the sleight of men, and cunning craftiness, whereby they lie in wait to deceive;
But speaking the truth in love, may grow up into him in all

1

things, which is the head, even Christ:
From whom the whole body fitly joined together and com-
pacted by that which every joint supplieth, according to
the effectual working in the measure of every part, maketh
increase of the body unto the edifying of itself in love.

Compare the body of Christ to a brick building. The
bricks would topple in the breeze if they were not joined
together. Mortar forms those bricks into a solid,
impenetrable wall. However, it is *held together*, or made
useful, by the *effectual working in the measure of every part.*
The power of love, through prayer and intercession is
the mortar which knits the Body together.

Each member contributes his part by building up the
Body and strengthening it through prayer. If one is
injured or weakened in some way, the others are able to
stand in prayer and make up for that weakness.

Prayer and Fellowship

Faith causes your prayers to bring results. Faith
pleases God (Heb. 11:6). It pleases Him to answer your
prayers. He can only manifest Himself in the earth
through the believer who is operating in faith. *However,*
there will be no strong faith without a deep and intimate
fellowship with the Father. This is the very heart of a
successful prayer life.

Fellowship is the mother of faith. You can only put
your faith and confidence in God to the extent that you
know Him. By spending time in fellowship with Him,
you will become personally acquainted with your
heavenly Father.

Your new birth into the family of God gave you the
right to expect your prayers to be answered. You came
into a Father-child relationship. *Relationship without*
fellowship, however, is like marriage without love. In a

2

loveless marriage, two people are related but don't really know each other.

If I never spent quality time fellowshipping with my son, anyone could tell him lies about me and he would believe them. The same thing applies to a husband and wife, an employer and an employee, business partners, etc. Lack of fellowship causes lack of trust. If that can happen in human relationships it can happen between my heavenly Father and me.

By not fellowshipping with God, you will come to a place where Satan could lie to you about God—he would say God is your problem or He is the One making you sick to teach you something. You will believe it. You will not have a *personal experience* with the Father, called trust (faith), that refuses the lies of Satan called doubt (unbelief). Consequently, you will not resist those lies but begin to accept them as truth. *Thou wilt keep him in perfect peace, whose mind is stayed on thee: because he trusteth in thee* (Is. 26:3).

God is NOT your problem. The more you fellowship with Him, the more you know that He is FOR you. He wants to use His power in your behalf. Galatians 1:3,4 says, *Grace be to you and peace from God the Father, and from our Lord Jesus Christ, Who gave Himself for our sins, that He might deliver us from this present evil world, according to the will of God and our Father.*

The number one priority in God's heart is to spend **quality time** with us everyday. As believers, we need to be able to hear His voice and follow the promptings of the Holy Spirit. We have the command to resist anything that does not come from Him (James 4:7). God does not want us lacking in any area of our lives.

> *I thank my God always on your behalf, for the grace of God which is given you by Jesus Christ;*
> *That in every thing ye are enriched by him, in all utterance, and in all knowledge;*

3

*Even as the testimony of Christ was confirmed in you:
So that ye come behind in no gift; waiting for the coming
of our Lord Jesus Christ:
Who shall also confirm you unto the end, that ye
may be blameless in the day of our Lord Jesus Christ.
God is faithful, by whom ye were called unto the
fellowship of his Son Jesus Christ our Lord.*

1 Corinthians 1:4-9

When you heed that call to fellowship you will find out for *yourself* that **God is faithful.** Your life will be enhanced by Him. You will not come behind in any area.

Fellowship is so vitally important. It will cause you to operate out of your spirit where the faith and power of God reside. Mere head knowledge of the Word, or what is called mental assent, will not cause you to tap into the power of God. Mental assent is simply agreeing that God's Word is true. On the other hand, fellowship will bring you to a place of operating out of *revelation knowledge.* When you know, that you know, that you know, that God's promise is good, **nothing** can take it away from you! All fear and doubt are dispelled.

By maintaining a consistent and close fellowship with God, you will bear fruit in your life. *Abide in me, and I in you. As the branch cannot bear fruit of itself, except it abide in the vine; no more can ye, except ye abide in me. I am the vine, ye are the branches: He that abideth in me, and I in him, the same bringeth forth much fruit: for without me ye can do nothing. … If ye abide in me, and my words abide in you, ye shall ask what ye will, and it shall be done unto you* (John 15:4,5,7). Jesus said, *Herein is my Father glorified, that ye bear much fruit; so shall ye be my disciples.* Bearing fruit is doing the works of Jesus; consequently pleasing the Father.

Now the God of peace…Make you perfect in every good work to do his will, working in you that which is well-pleasing in his sight (Heb. 13:20,21). This is a clear example of God's will for every believer. When you are perfect in every good work, doing His will, pleasing Him, you bear fruit.

Notice Colossians 1:9,10, ...*we...do not cease to pray for you, and to desire that ye might be filled with the knowledge of his will in all wisdom and spiritual understanding; That ye might walk worthy of the Lord unto all pleasing, being fruitful in every good work, and increasing in the knowledge of God.* The better you know God, the more fruitful you become. Fellowship causes you to bear fruit by *His* power working in you and not by your own power.

The way to bear fruit is by prayer. Jesus always separated Himself from people to spend time in prayer. He had a personal relationship with the Father. He stayed in tune with the Holy Spirit through fellowship and prayer.

Set aside time everyday to spend with your heavenly Father. Make the decision that you will not allow *anything* to interfere with your quality time alone with Him.

The more time you spend in His presence, the more you will act and think like Him. God has already given you His nature. Fellowshipping with Him will cause your attitudes, actions and beliefs to line up. The more time you spend with your Father in the Word, the more your desires will become His desires. Then when you pray, you will simply be voicing His will. The reality of God will burn into your consciousness. You will not be crying out to God 92,000 miles away. He will be right there—closer than a brother. As you draw nigh unto God, He will draw nigh unto you (James 4:8). No danger in this world, no circumstance, no problem can come near you with God Almighty by your side!

Fellowshipping with God on a personal basis will give birth to a deep, strong faith and trust in His ability. Your prayer life will take on new meaning.

As a born-again believer, you have everything that you need to succeed in this life. God is a winner! You are His very own child. You have been born again to win! When you are praying in faith and confidence, all of heaven's resources are at your disposal! Determine in your heart that you will maintain consistent and intimate fellowship with God so that your prayer life will be based on *personal knowledge* of Him.

Chapter II
Praying for Results

Regardless of any man's ability, he will fail if his endeavors are not backed by prayer. The major cause of failure in Christian enterprises is an omission of prayer.

Whether your goal is to witness to one man or to preach the Gospel to nations, you will succeed or fail based entirely on your prayer life. One percent of your time spent in prayer will produce only one percent results. Eighty percent prayer will bring 80 percent results. This formula works every time. The obvious question is, "But how can I expect to receive 100 percent results? I can't spend all of my time in prayer." Oh yes, you can!

Prayer is an attitude. It involves more than just making requests. Prayer is communicating with God. You can live in an attitude of prayer constantly, being in communion and fellowship with your heavenly Father every hour of the day.

In order to get results in prayer, you must be convinced of one basic fact: **God wants to answer your prayers.** In fact, He is as ready and willing to answer you as He was to answer Jesus during His earthly ministry. This may be difficult for you to believe, but it is true.

I remember how amazed I was to learn about God's willingness to answer my prayers. I had always thought of myself as unworthy. I thought, *Why would God bother to answer my prayers?* Ignorance of God's Word kept me from receiving His best in my life.

Once I realized the importance of the Word of God, my attitude changed. I realized that God does not see His children as unworthy. Notice how Jesus prayed: ... *that the world may know that thou hast sent me, and hast loved them, as thou hast loved me* (John 17:23). Just think! God loves you and me as much as He loves Jesus! **We are worthy!**

Knowing that God is ready to answer your prayers will make you serious about your prayer life. Never take your prayer privilege lightly. Because you are a child of God, you have an open invitation from Him to come into the throne room any time you wish. You do not have to enter His presence crawling on your hands and knees. You can boldly stand before God without a sense of guilt or shame or condemnation.

Let us therefore come boldly unto the throne of grace, that we may obtain mercy, and find grace to help in time of need (Heb. 4:16).

What is Prayer?

To understand what prayer is, it helps to realize what it is not. Prayer is not an emotional release. It is not an escape valve. It is much more than just asking God for a favor. Perhaps most important of all, prayer is not a religious exercise.

You should be praying for results every time you pray. Do not just speak empty words. Jesus said in Matthew 6:7:

But when ye pray, use not vain repetitions, as the heathen do: for they think that they shall be heard for their much speaking.

The beauty of your prayer does not get the ear of God. He responds to faith. To explain, let me give you an example from my own experience.

Not long after I became a Christian, I asked a minister to pray for me. I was expecting to hear a long, beautiful prayer—one that would cause people to fall on their knees in repentance before God! What I heard was just the opposite. He laid his hand on my chest, bowed his head, and said, "Lord, bless him. Meet his every need." He then turned and walked away. I was left standing there thinking "How could he do that to me? I have big problems. It should have taken at least twenty minutes of hard praying to cover everything."

One major difference separated that minister and me: the degree of faith at work in our lives. He was operating in faith, praying exactly what he meant. I was a baby Christian, looking for a physical manifestation of some kind.

It makes no difference how long you pray or how beautiful your words. **Praying in faith is merely having confidence in God's willingness to use His power to answer your prayer.**

The man who knows the importance of prayer is very difficult to defeat. He knows that, regardless of what comes, he can pray and God will move in his behalf.

The key to success in prayer is expecting results. Many Christians think, "I'll pray and maybe something will happen." They say, "I'm just hoping and praying."

If you are hoping to get results, you will never receive from God. "Hoping to get" is not the same as "believing you receive." The promises of God bring you hope in hopeless situations. However, hope has no substance in itself. "I hope to get healed someday." You hope to receive someday, but someday never comes. **Faith brings hope into reality and gives**

9

substance to it. Hebrews 11:1 says: *Now faith is the substance of things hoped for, the evidence of things not seen.* The object of hope becomes a reality through faith. Hope is always in the future. Faith is always *now*.

Faith causes you to receive from God. The believer who is operating in faith believes that God's power went to work the moment he prayed.

God's Word in Prayer

The number one rule in praying for results is: base your prayer on God's Word. It can be relied on just as you would depend on the word of your best friend. If you trust him, you will believe what he says. Faith in God operates the same way. **God's Word is the integrity of God Himself** (John 17:17).

As an example, let's use the prayer for salvation. Your first step is to go to the Word and find out what God says you must do to be saved. Romans 10:9,10 says, *That if thou shalt confess with thy mouth the Lord Jesus, and shalt believe in thine heart that God hath raised him from the dead, thou shalt be saved. For with the heart man believeth unto righteousness; and with the mouth confession is made unto salvation.*

This scripture is the basis for your prayer. You confess with your mouth Jesus as Lord and you believe in your heart that God has raised Him from the dead. God's Word says it so you can accept it as fact. When you fulfill these two prerequisites, the Word says, *Thou shalt be saved.* You must receive it by faith.

When you pray the prayer of salvation, you may not feel differently. Realize that your feelings do not have anything to do with it. **God's Word is His part of your prayer life.** He has already said in His Word, *Thou shalt be saved.* You have allowed the Word of God to engineer your prayer. It makes no difference how you feel. Exercise your faith. By the authority of God's Word you are saved! In Mark 11:24 Jesus said, *What things soever ye desire, when ye pray, believe that ye receive them, and ye shall have them.*

God's Word is His will. When you pray in line with the Word, you have automatically prayed in line with God's will. First John 5:14,15 says, *And this is the confidence that we have in him, that, if we ask any thing according to his will, he heareth us: And if we know that he hear us, whatsoever we ask, we know that we have the petitions that we desired of him.* Your prayer for salvation, based on God's Word, was clearly heard by the Father. After you pray and receive your salvation by faith, you then simply thank God for it.

Second Corinthians 5:17 says, *If any man be in Christ, he is a new creature: old things are passed away; behold, all things are become new.* See yourself as a new creation. Visualize that the man you once were died the death of the cross and was raised to new life by the power of the Holy Spirit (Rom. 6:4). This is actually what happened. You prayed according to the Word of God, therefore you are saved.

Praying for healing involves the same faith principles. Search God's Word for your answer.

Isaiah 53:5 says, *But he was wounded for our transgressions, he was bruised for our iniquities: the chastisement of our peace was upon him; and with his stripes we are healed.* Matthew 8:17 says, *Himself took our infirmities, and bare our sicknesses.* Undoubtedly healing is God's will. According to these scriptures, Jesus paid the full price—not only for sin, but for sickness, disease and the consequences of sin.

More religious traditions have discounted God's will for healing than those that discredit salvation. To know God's will toward healing, look at Jesus. Jesus said, *He that hath seen me hath seen the Father* (John 14:9). During

11

His time on earth, Jesus was the express image of God (Heb. 1:3). What did He do? He healed the sick. Acts 10:38 says, *God anointed Jesus of Nazareth with the Holy Ghost and with power: who went about doing good, and healing all that were oppressed of the devil; for God was with him.*

The prayer for healing is a simple one. You say, "Father, in the name of Jesus, I see in Your Word that healing belongs to me. I believe I receive it. I thank You for it. I act upon it now." Once you have prayed, TRUST. Do not let Satan convince you that you are still sick. He will try his best to sell you his lies. **Stand your ground!** Say, "Satan, it is written...." Then begin to speak what God's Word says about your healing. Just as he fled at the command of Jesus' words, Satan will have to flee when you speak God's Word in faith (Matt. 4:1-11). He has no defense against the Word of God when it is spoken in faith by a believer.

Applying Faith in Prayer

When you begin your prayer based on God's Word, you are starting with the answer. The Word contains the answer to every problem that could confront you.

The next step in praying effectively is found in Mark 11:22-24. Jesus said, *What things soever ye desire, when ye pray, believe that ye receive them, and ye shall have them.* This places a qualification on your prayer. You have to believe you receive *when you pray.* Do not wait until the manifestation comes to believe you receive.

This will seem very difficult at first. But as you get to know God personally, you will become convinced that His Word is true. The problem area will diminish. **Make a quality decision to believe God's Word.** Numbers 23:19 says:

God is not a man, that he should lie; neither the son of man, that he should repent: hath he said, and shall he not do it? or hath he spoken, and shall he not make it good? You can trust His integrity. When you pray, all you have to do is apply your faith.

Where does faith come from? How do you get faith? Faith comes by hearing, and hearing by the Word of God (Rom. 10:17). Every believer is dealt the measure of faith (Rom. 12:3). He must develop that faith by spending time in the Word of God. The application of your faith in any given situation is directly related to your knowledge of God. You could not have faith to be saved before you knew it was God's will to save you. If you feel that you need more faith, realize that you already have faith. What you need is a more personal knowledge of God through time in the Word.

Once you have prayed in faith, hold fast to your confession. God is aware of your situation. His power went to work the instant you prayed in faith. You can now rest assured that what you prayed will come to pass. *Maintain* your faith by keeping your confession in line with the Word.

There remaineth therefore a rest to the people of God. For he that is entered into his rest, he also hath ceased from his own works, as God did from his. Let us labour therefore to enter into that rest, lest any man fall after the same example of unbelief. For the word of God is quick, and powerful, and sharper than any twoedged sword, piercing even to the dividing asunder of soul and spirit, and of the joints and marrow, and is a discerner of the thoughts and intents of the heart. Neither is there any creature that is not manifest in his sight: but all things are naked and opened unto the eyes of him with whom we have to do. Seeing then that we have a great high priest, that is passed into the heavens, Jesus the Son of God, let us hold fast our profession (Heb. 4:9-14). Speak only words that agree with what you desire. Jesus is seated at the right hand of the Father. As your High Priest, He is seeing to it that the whole system works the way God said it would!

The importance of speaking right words cannot be measured. Faith is released with the mouth. Words are the vehicles. God spoke faith-filled words when He created the universe. Hebrews 11:3 says, *Through faith we understand that the worlds were framed by the word of God.* God spoke and the Spirit of God used the faith in those words to create the worlds.

Even Jesus ministered during His earthly ministry by speaking words. At the tomb of Lazarus, He *said, Lazarus, come forth,* and he did. At the city of Nain, Jesus stopped a funeral procession and *said, My son, I say unto thee, arise.* The boy was raised from the dead. Matthew 8:16 says that Jesus cast out the devil with His Word. According to Psalm 107:20, God sent His Word and it healed the children of Israel.

Words carry power. The very power of life and death are in the tongue. Ask the Holy Spirit to reveal to you the gravity of speaking right things.

When faith words are spoken, they must be backed by corresponding actions. James 2:17, *Amplified Bible* says, *So also faith if it does not have works (deeds and actions of obedience to back it up), by itself is destitute of power—inoperative, dead.* God's Word instructs us to be doers and not hearers only. In applying faith, two elements are involved: words *and* actions. **Real Bible faith demands action.**

You have to *act by faith, not according to your feelings or reasonings.* Faith is based on eternal truth and is more dependable than the evidence of your physical senses. According to 2 Corinthians 4:18, we are not to look at things which are seen, but at things which are not seen. The things which are visible are temporal, or changeable. The things which are invisible are eternal, they never change. Don't focus your attention on what you perceive through your five physical senses. Keep your heart fixed on the Word of God. Then what you see will come in line with the Word.

To believe God's Word rather than physical circumstances is to talk and act the answer instead of the problem. **Acting on the Word puts faith into motion.** You cannot expect results from your prayer without the operation of faith.

One incident that occurred during the ministry of Jesus, is a fine example of faith in action. Jesus was teaching in a private home. The crowd was so large there was no room for anyone else. Some men had brought a sick friend to Jesus to be healed. When they could not reach Him because of the throng of people, they refused to be denied. They knocked a hole in the roof and lowered him into the room on a stretcher.

The owner of that house thought as much of his roof as you think of yours. How do you suppose he reacted when they tore a hole in his roof? These men had one thing in mind: to reach Jesus. They put aside their own dignity and refused to fear the owner of the house or the people around them. When they lowered the sick man into the room, Luke 5:20 says that **Jesus SAW their faith.** The invisible force of faith became visible through their actions! In response to faith, Jesus forgave the man's sins and healed his body.

What Jesus did 2,000 years ago, He will do today. He is the same yesterday, today, and forever (Heb. 13:8).

Once you have prayed, hold fast to your confession. Refuse to speak contrary to the Word of God. Do not allow circumstances to sway you. **Act as though it were already done.**

When you apply your faith accurately according to God's Word, you *will* get results. You will experience Hebrews 4:16 for yourself. *Let us therefore come boldly unto the throne of grace, that we may obtain mercy, and find grace to help in time of need.* It does not say, "Come and hope to get." It says, "Come **obtain!**"

A very misunderstood concept throughout the religious world is that it is extremely difficult to get God to answer prayer at all—much less answer all prayer. That is a lie of Satan and absolutely contrary to the Word of God. **When you believe God's Word in your heart and you pray in line with His Word, you have every right to expect your prayer to bring results.** Jesus said:

Verily I say unto you, If ye have faith, and doubt not, ye shall not only do this which is done to the fig tree, but also if ye shall say unto this mountain, Be thou removed, and be thou cast into the sea; it shall be done.

And all things, whatsoever ye shall ask in prayer, believing, ye shall receive.

Matthew 21:21,22

If God will answer the prayer of a sinner to be saved, He will certainly answer the prayers of born-again believers who come to Him in faith concerning their lives.

Refusing Doubt

Satan uses doubt with great skill and cunning to cause you to fail. He knows the importance of getting you to waiver. He constantly tries to throw doubt and unbelief into your consciousness. If you begin to wonder whether you have the answer, Satan will purpose to secure a foothold in your mind. By gradually increasing his influence, your faith will not be effective. This will cause you to be defeated.

Matthew 14:24-31 is a perfect illustration. Jesus' disciples were traveling to the other side of the sea by ship.

But the ship was now in the midst of the sea, tossed with waves: for the wind was contrary.

And in the fourth watch of the night Jesus went unto them, walking on the sea. And when the disciples saw him walking on the sea, they were troubled, saying, It is a spirit; and they cried out for fear.

But straightway Jesus spake unto them saying, Be of good cheer; it is I; be not afraid.

And Peter answered him and said, Lord, if it be thou, bid me come unto thee on the water. And he said, Come.

And when Peter was come down out of the ship, he walked on the water, to go to Jesus. But when he saw the wind boisterous, he was afraid; and beginning to sink, he cried, saying, Lord, save me.

And immediately Jesus stretched forth his hand, and caught him, and said unto him, O thou of little faith, wherefore didst thou doubt?

When Peter cried out to Jesus, He answered him with one word: "Come." That command carried the authority necessary to defy all natural power. Faith supported him on the water. Peter stepped out of the boat into a supernatural experience. When he *saw* the wind, however, he became *afraid* and failed. **He saw, he feared, and he sank!**

Three elements are always involved in defeat:

SEE + FEAR + DOUBT = DEFEATED FAITH

Doubt was the thief that robbed Peter of God's best. Great sermons have been made about how Jesus was there to save him. God's best was not that he be rescued in the nick of time before he was overwhelmed by a raging sea! Peter had an opportunity to walk in the supernatural in spite of what was happening in the natural. *Faith or fear*—you can not be functioning in both at the same time. Doubt causes defeat!

In praying effectively, a vital part of your success is knowing how to refuse doubt, fear, and unbelief. If you are concentrating on your circumstances instead of the Word, you are building an inner image of the problem and not the solution. What you see on the inside will

17

determine your attitude. If all you envision is your negative circumstances, you will doubt God's Word. Satan will take advantage of you to thwart your faith process.

Doubt operates in the mental realm. God's Word operates in the spiritual realm. Our responsibility is to use the spiritual weapons at our disposal. *For though we walk in the flesh, we do not war after the flesh: (For the weapons of our warfare are not carnal, but mighty through God to the pulling down of strong holds;) Casting down imaginations, and every high thing that exalteth itself against the knowledge of God, and bringing into captivity every thought to the obedience of Christ...* (2 Cor. 10:3-5). Peter's battle was not with natural forces. The combat was spiritual. Natural law was subject to the power inherent in Jesus' word, *come.* By stepping out of the boat, Peter acted on the authority in that word.

We can walk in the supernatural in spite of life's storms raging against us. Our spiritual weapons are *mighty!*

Maintain control of your mind. Do not allow doubt or fear to enter your consciousness. Be ready to refuse any thought or imagination contrary to your prayer. When doubt comes, refuse to give it any place. Be selective about the thoughts you entertain. Do not build inner images of defeat! Control your thought-life according to Philippians 4:6-9. Learn to think on things that are true, honest, just, pure, lovely, and of good report.

Satan uses doubt and fear to bluff you into accepting defeat. You can overcome him by the power of God and faith in His Word.

Prepare to Succeed

You can avoid failure by *preparing* to succeed. Once you have prayed in faith, you must **stand your ground until the manifestation comes.** Fight the good fight of faith. Stand firm on the Word and believe God for results. Give Him the opportunity to do something with your circumstances. God is on *your* side! Prepare to succeed, not to fail.

When you pray in Jesus' name, according to the Word in faith, God will quickly respond to you (John 16:23).

Suppose you prayed for healing. Then you think, "What will I do if God doesn't heal me? Maybe I had better get an appointment with the doctor. He's awfully busy this time of year. I might not be able to see him. Then if God doesn't heal me, I'll be in a mess!"

With that attitude, believing God will be a waste of time. The person who thinks that way will be unable to receive from God. Before he prays, he is already preparing to fail. He is double minded and, according to James 1:8, unstable in all his ways. *The man who waivers in his mind will never receive from God.* He is like a wave of the sea, driven with the wind and tossed about in every direction. He has a back-up plan "just in case." The moment he feels the least bit sick, he will operate in fear and unbelief. When he feels well, he will act in faith, but he will never achieve any concrete results.

If the thought comes, *But what am I going to do if I fail?* Don't give place to it. If you have a setback, just get back on the Word of God. The power of God is the same whether you feel like it or not. Receive the Word into your heart. Renew your mental attitude to the Word. Prepare to succeed and you will receive the manifestation in the physical realm.

You may ask, "But how do I prepare to succeed?" Keep your attention on God's Word. Look at Proverbs 4:20-22: *My son, attend to my words; incline thine ear unto my sayings. Let them not depart from thine eyes; keep them in the midst of thine heart. For they are life unto those that find them, and health to all their flesh.*

Do not listen to the voice of circumstances around you. Keep the Word of God before you. Do whatever is necessary to keep Satan and circumstances under control. If that means reading the Word 200 times a day, then do it!

Jesus said in Matthew 6:22, *The light of the body is the eye: if therefore thine eye be single, thy whole body shall be full of light.* Your body responds to what it is fed through the eyes. If you are believing God for healing, you must feed your consciousness with the Word of God which will bring healing. Waste no time on useless activities. Be diligent to spend your time in God's Word. **The Word of God will set you free. Make plans to succeed!**

Together, these principles will to bring the desired result: the manifestation of answered prayer by God's supernatural power. At that moment, you have a realization of God's ability from your own personal experience, not just through another's testimony. This is probably the most exciting thing that could happen. You realize God moved because *you* prayed and used your faith.

The day Gloria and I were married was a beautiful experience in my life. Much more than that have been the experiences we have had in believing God together, watching Him move when we pray. To know that God sees us and cares about us, about our family, about the circumstances around us has truly enhanced our lives. *You have never lived until you know the thrill of watching your prayers come to pass!*

Chapter III
The Battlefield of Prayer

Finally, my brethren, be strong in the Lord, and in the power of his might.

Put on the whole armour of God, that ye may be able to stand against the wiles of the devil.

For we wrestle not against flesh and blood, but against principalities, against powers, against the rulers of the darkness of this world, against spiritual wickedness in high places.

Wherefore take unto you the whole armour of God, that ye may be able to withstand in the evil day, and having done all, to stand.

Stand therefore, having your loins girt about with truth, and having on the breastplate of righteousness; And your feet shod with the preparation of the gospel of peace; Above all, taking the shield of faith, wherewith ye shall be able to quench all the fiery darts of the wicked. And take the helmet of salvation, and the sword of the Spirit, which is the word of God:

Praying always with all prayer and supplication in the Spirit....

Ephesians 6:10-18

Every believer is involved in spiritual warfare. The problems we face are brought about by satanic forces —principalities, powers, rulers of the darkness of this world and wicked spirits in heavenly places. Our responsibility is to use the weapons of our warfare to fight the good fight of faith. What are those weapons?

The name of Jesus, the Word of God, the Holy Spirit and the gifts of the Spirit.

Prayer is the battlefield. The time spent in prayer is the base of supply. The armor described in Ephesians, chapter six is prayer armor. It serves one vital purpose: to combat Satan and win!

Your enemy is not other people. Satan is the source of all your trouble. Some people believe that *God* sends tribulation and trials. But God has provided the weapons and armor that get us out of trouble! Satan is the troublemaker! Not God! Not your neighbor! Not your co-worker!

In combat a good strategist knows the importance of cutting the enemy's supply and dividing his troops. Defeat is inevitable. Without a supply of food, water, and ammunition, it will be only a matter of time until the enemy is in his hands. In fact, all he has to do is sit back and wait. If we are not spending time in prayer actively combating Satan, then he can easily overtake us.

Satan's strategy is to move in and cut off our supply. Much of our failure in the past has been Satan's success in dividing the church. But thank God, the body of Christ is coming together throughout the earth. People of all denominational backgrounds are uniting in the power of the Holy Spirit. Believers are discovering more and more each day the power of God that is available to them. They are putting on their prayer armor, preparing to do battle in the world of the spirit. The barriers of denominations are crumbling like the walls of Jericho!

Thank God, we have authority over Satan and his cohorts. We are to be strong in the Lord and in the power of His might. We must master our weapons and use them effectively. If we expect to win the war, we must spend the time to reinforce our troops through prayer.

The Whole Armor of God

As a believer, you are a soldier in the army of God. Visualize yourself standing ready for battle with the armor of God protecting you—your loins girt with the truth. The breastplate of righteousness is in place. Your feet are shod with the preparation of the Gospel of peace. ABOVE ALL, you are holding the shield of faith to quench ALL the fiery darts of the wicked. You have the helmet of salvation on your head and the sword of the Spirit—the Word of God—in your hand.

You are covered head to foot with the powerful armor of God. It is strong and will withstand any onslaught of the enemy. Let me show you how it works.

And having done all, to stand. Stand therefore, having your loins girt about with truth. When Satan tells you in your mind that you will never see the manifestation of your prayers, that is the time to gird yourself with the truth. Jesus said, *Thy* (God's Word) *word is truth* (John 17:17). Satan is the liar and father of lies. Determine in your heart that having done all to stand, you will stand firm on God's Word. You will not be moved by what you see, hear or think. You are only moved by the Word of God.

Of the man who delights in God's Word, making it final authority, Psalm 112:6-8 says:

Surely he shall not be moved for ever: the righteous shall be in everlasting remembrance.

He shall not be afraid of evil tidings: his heart is fixed, trusting in the Lord.

His heart is established, he shall not be afraid, until he see his desire upon his enemies.

Fix your attention on God's Word. Trust only in the Lord and not in the evil reports you hear. Establish your heart in the Word of God!

The breastplate of righteousness has a particular meaning to you as a believer. It was no accident that the

Spirit of God chose the breastplate to represent righteousness. Without the breastplate, vital areas of a soldier's body are exposed to his enemy. Without righteousness, the vital parts of your prayer life are exposed to Satan.

Righteousness may well be the most misunderstood subject in the New Testament. To the religious mind, righteousness is good moral conduct. The true meaning, however, is very different. *Righteousness* is simply right-standing with God. Because of that right-standing, you have rights and privileges in His kingdom.

You will become more aware of those rights and privileges as you realize what happens when you make Jesus the Lord of your life. There are two spiritual families: the family of God and the family of the devil. *For I reckon that the sufferings of this present time are not worthy to be compared with the glory which shall be revealed in us* (Rom. 8:18). *Ye are of your father the devil, and the lusts of your father ye will do. He was a murderer from the beginning, and abode not in the truth, because there is no truth in him. When he speaketh a lie, he speaketh of his own: for he is a liar, and the father of it* (John 8:44). *Wherein in time past ye walked according to the course of this world, according to the prince of the power of the air, the spirit that now worketh in the children of disobedience: Among whom also we all had our conversation in times past in the lusts of our flesh, fulfilling the desires of the flesh and of the mind; and were by nature the children of wrath, even as others* (Eph. 2:2,3). Your faith in Jesus gives you power to become a child of God. When you make Jesus the Lord of your life, your spirit is born again. You no longer belong to Satan's kingdom. You are translated into the kingdom of God's Son (Col. 1:12,13). **You are now an heir of God and a joint-heir with Jesus Christ! What is His is yours. You have His righteousness! This is your breastplate!** It makes you worthy in the sight of God.

As long as you see yourself unworthy, you will not experience answered prayer to any great degree. An understanding of righteousness will put you on the road to success. You have a right to resist Satan and expect him to flee.

Believers all over the world are learning their rights. They are becoming more and more aware of their position as children of God and joint-heirs with Jesus (Rom. 8:17). They are taking advantage of the breastplate of righteousness!

Your next piece of armor is for your feet. They are to be shod with the preparation of the Gospel of peace. Jesus said, *Go ye into all the world, and preach the gospel to every creature.* The Gospel is the Good News that we have peace through Jesus Christ. Isaiah 52:7 says, *How beautiful upon the mountains are the feet of him that bringeth good tidings, that publisheth peace.* Sharing the Gospel with others is part of your armor.

The Word says, *Above all, taking the shield of faith.* Your shield quenches *all* of the fiery darts of the wicked! First John 5:4 says, *And this is the victory that overcometh the world, even our faith.* Your faith makes you an overcomer and more than a conqueror! *The just shall live by faith* (Rom. 1:17). This means, your whole life is sustained by your faith in God.

Finally, *take the helmet of salvation.* A helmet is protection for the head. Romans 12:2 says, *And be not conformed to this world: but be ye transformed by the renewing of your mind, that ye may prove what is that good, and acceptable, and perfect, will of God.* Satan's battleground is your mind. By keeping your mind renewed to the Word of God, you will protect it from Satan's onslaught of doubt and unbelief. This is closely related to having your loins girt with the truth. Freedom is in the truth. Jesus said, *If ye continue in my word, then are ye my disciples indeed; And ye shall know the truth, and the truth shall make you free.* The key is *continuing.* You cannot just *try* this. You must make a quality decision to *do* it. You will then experience the freedom from Satan that is rightfully yours as a child of God.

Your armor is the same spiritual armor that Jesus wore during His earthly ministry. *And he saw that there was no man, and wondered that there was no intercessor: therefore his arm brought salvation unto him; and his righteousness, it sustained him. For he put on righteousness as a breastplate, and an helmet of salvation upon his head; and he put on the garments of vengeance for clothing, and was clad with zeal as a cloak* (Is. 59:16,17). He proved it before He gave it to you. It worked proficiently for Him. Why? Because He was here for one purpose—to fulfill God's will in the earth. Jesus ministered on earth as a prophet under the Abrahamic covenant. Philippians 2:8 says that Jesus humbled Himself. In the original Greek, that literally says, *He emptied Himself of His divine privileges.* He walked as a man, filled with the Holy Ghost. Jesus said, *I can of mine own self do nothing: as I hear, I judge: and my judgment is just; because I seek not mine own will, but the will of the Father which hath sent me* (John 5:30). He wore this armor as a *man* and then He gave it to the church!

God has set in motion a security system on earth. This system is prayer. It includes the whole armor of God *and* the weapons of our warfare. The principles involved are designed to put a padlock on Satan's forces. This gives the Spirit of God an avenue through which He can carry out God's will in the lives of His people.

The Weapons of Our Warfare

The armor we have talked about has been defensive. Let's look at our offensive weapons! Ephesians 6:17 says that the Word of God is the sword of the Spirit. To handle your sword skillfully, you need to know how the Word works. It will bring results. Satan will retreat from its blows in terror!

In Mark four, Jesus likens the Word of God to seed sown in the ground. When you plant seed, it produces a crop. You do not plant corn, expecting to grow apples or bananas. When corn is planted, corn will grow. So it is with the Word of God. When you plant the Word in your heart, it will grow and produce.

Your life—like soil—will produce what is sown in it. Plant seeds of doubt, fear, unbelief, and failure and you can expect to produce a crop of doubt, fear, unbelief, and failure in your life. You cannot plant seeds of doubt expecting to produce faith. It simply will not work.

The Word is sharper than a two-edged sword, piercing and dividing asunder the soul and the spirit, the joints and the marrow (Heb. 4:12). The Word goes beyond your intellect. It enters the spirit realm. Only doubt and unbelief will stop the Word from operating in your behalf. When you plant the Word concerning healing in your heart, then you will produce a harvest of healing IF doubt and fear do not enter and ruin your crop.

Jesus said, *The sower soweth the word...but when they have heard, Satan cometh immediately, and taketh away the word that was sown in their hearts.* Satan comes *immediately* to steal the Word. You have to guard against his maneuvers. The best way to combat an enemy is to familiarize yourself with his tactics. Once you know how Satan operates, you will be able to defeat him.

When a man plants seed in the ground, he does not go out a few days later and dig it up to see if it is growing. Seeds never produce that way. He has to have faith in the seed's ability to grow and produce.

Faith in the Word works the same way. When you are believing God for healing, and the symptoms linger, you do not give up and say, "Well, I guess it didn't work for me." That's what Satan would like you to do. You have to continually water the ground and cultivate it with the Word until the seed is able to sprout and grow. Don't dig up your seed!

If a farmer placed his seed on a shelf, it would never produce. He must put the seed in its correct environment for the life in it to come forth. The Word must be treated as that seed. If you need healing, then plant the seed of God's Word concerning healing in the correct environment—your heart. When your Bible is left lying on a bookshelf, it will be of no use to you.

Not spending time in the Word when you are fighting a spiritual battle would be like leaving your sword in its sheath while you are on the battlefield. Take your Bible down from the shelf and feed the Word into your heart. Spend time meditating in the Word until the seed of healing can grow and develop and bring forth the desired fruit in your life.

When a seed is planted in the ground and cultivated, it will take root. The shoot will force its way to the surface. When the plant blooms, it will produce many more just like it. **The Word, like a seed, has the power within itself to grow and bear fruit.**

Protect the Word until it has time to take root and grow. Rule over your thought life by casting down imaginations that exalt themselves against the Word. To be carnally minded or sense-ruled is death (Rom. 8:6). It will kill you. To be spiritually minded is *life* and peace. Keep your thoughts on the Word. It is the answer to your problem. You will experience life and peace by keeping the end result on your mind and thus protecting the seed of God's Word. The Word of God works only when it is put to work. Submit yourselves to God (James 4:7). Resist the devil and he WILL flee from you!

God has provided a strong arsenal for spiritual warfare. The Word is not your only weapon against Satan.

In chapter one, we discussed briefly that every believer has the privilege of using the name of Jesus in prayer.

When you pray in Jesus' name, you immediately get the ear of God. At the same time, you get Satan's attention.

The name of Jesus carries ultimate authority in the spirit world. Philippians 2:9,10 says, ...*God also hath highly exalted him, and given him a name which is above every name: That at the name of Jesus every knee should bow, of things in heaven, and things in earth, and things under the earth.* In Jesus' name, the believer has authority to *tread on serpents and scorpions and over all the power of the enemy* (Luke 10:19). Satan knows the power invested in that name and he will retreat when it is spoken in faith (James 4:7). One translation says to stand up to the devil and he will turn and run!

Let's look at Hebrews 1:3,4: *Who being the brightness of his glory, and the express image of his person, and upholding all things by the word of his power, when he had by himself purged our sins, sat down on the right hand of the Majesty on high; Being made so much better than the angels, as he hath by inheritance obtained a more excellent name than they.* If the name of Jesus is more excellent than that of the angels in good-standing with God, how much more would it be than the name of Satan? He is a fallen angel!

Before He ascended into heaven, Jesus commissioned His disciples to go into all the earth. He said, "All power has been given unto me both in heaven and in earth. Therefore, YOU go into all the earth. IN MY NAME lay hands on the sick and they will recover. IN MY NAME cast out the devil." Just as a wife has power of attorney to her husband's name, we have been given Jesus' name to use in combat against Satan. We have authority to speak His name in His stead.

When Peter and John ministered to the man at the Gate Beautiful, they spoke in the name of Jesus. Peter said, *Silver and gold have I none; but such as I have give I thee: In the name of Jesus Christ of Nazareth rise up and walk.* Later he explained what had happened. Peter said, *Ye men of Israel, why marvel ye at this? or why look ye so earnestly on us, as though by our own power or holiness we had made this man to walk? The God of Abraham, and of Isaac, and of Jacob, the God of our fathers, hath glorified his Son Jesus...And his name through faith in his name hath made this man strong, whom ye see and know: yea, the faith which is by him hath given him this perfect soundness in the presence of you all* (Acts 3:6,12,13,16).

Peter was simply using the authority Jesus had given him only a few days before. The early apostles did not have special power in themselves to do mighty works. Their holiness didn't make them special. They didn't even have the written New Testament. All they could do was speak Jesus' name in faith and the Holy Spirit did the mighty works. The fabulous earth-shaking revival of the early church was sparked by only one commandment: "Go in the name of Jesus." The power invested in Jesus' name has *never* changed.

Most believers know that it is the name of Jesus that caused them to be saved. The Bible says, *Whosoever shall call upon his name shall be saved. He is rich unto those that call upon his name.* When you call upon someone's name, you are placing a demand on their ability. For instance, when a policeman says, "Halt in the name of the law!", he is being backed by the power of that particular city. It is as if the entire corporate structure of that city is speaking. He is carrying out the power behind the name of the law.

To know how much confidence you can place in a name, you must be able to measure the power behind it. A man writing a check, places a demand on his name. If he has the proper funds in the bank, then there is enough power to meet the demand.

The power backing the name of Jesus is the power of Almighty God! First John 3:22,23 says, *And whatsoever we ask, we receive of him, because we keep his commandments, and do those things that are pleasing in his sight. And this is his commandment, That we should believe on the name of his Son Jesus Christ, and love one another, as he gave us commandment.* We have a commandment to believe on the name of the Son of God. To believe on His name is to put demand upon His ability. Jesus said, *Whatsoever ye shall ask the Father in my name, he will give it you* (John 16:23). The mighty, powerful name of Jesus is available to you. Become aware of your right and privilege to use it. Ask the Holy Spirit to engrave the reality of it in your heart. His ministry is to lead you into *all* truth (John 16:13).

The name of Jesus is the key to the heaven's storehouse. It can do anything that Jesus can do. Speaking His name is standing in His stead. According to Philippians 2:9-11, the entire spectrum of existence —heaven, earth, under the earth—will bow its knee and confess with its mouth that Jesus is Lord to the glory of God the Father. The name of Jesus is a name that is above every name. Upon being raised from the dead, Jesus inherited the very name of God (Heb. 1:4). To measure the power behind His name, you would have to measure the power of Almighty God. It cannot be done. His power is measureless and He wants to use it in our behalf.

God's love motivates Him to use His power. First John 4:16 says, *And we have known and believed the love that God hath to us.* When you *believe* the love that God has for you, then you will begin to realize that *you* have as much right to use the name of Jesus as any one else. Believe the love that God has for you.

Once you recognize the reality of God's love in your life, you will realize that He has not left you defenseless and powerless against evil. God covered the entire spectrum of Satan's existence with the power invested in the mighty name of Jesus. Use it freely and confidently in the face of your adversary!

Another essential aspect of our spiritual warfare is the Holy Spirit. Before He went to the cross, Jesus promised to send Him. We have armor, and weapons but it is the Holy Spirit who empowers us to utilize them.

The Holy Spirit is the power of God. The effectiveness of your prayer life depends on the degree of confidence you place in the Holy Spirit. He is the power behind your prayers that enables you to live and walk as God intends—free from sin, sickness, sorrow and death. He dwells within you. You may not be aware of His presence, but He is there. The Holy Spirit fills a vital role in your prayer life. Pray to the Father in Jesus' name, not to the Holy Spirit. He is in you—creating, energizing, working —to perform the will of God in your life. By operating on the Word of God, you will see the work of the Holy Spirit. He will do exceedingly abundantly beyond what we can even ask or think according to the power that is at work within us (Eph. 3:20). The Holy Spirit *is* that power.

He is your Helper, sent to bear you up. He has come to your aid to give you might in your inner man. He is in you, instantly ready to do the bidding of God and uphold the name of Jesus.

The operation of the Holy Spirit should be a reality to you. When you invite Him into your life, you receive more than just an experience. The Holy Spirit of God came to abide with you forever. He is residing inside you constantly. He is real and He wants to help you in your prayer life.

"Father, I ask You now to fill me with Your precious Holy Spirit. As He gives me the utterance, I will speak with new tongues, my own personal prayer language. I will practice praying in tongues, praying in the spirit, daily. I will do my part to exercise my new language and depend on the Holy Spirit to lead and guide me as I grow in You.

"Thank You, Father, for filling me with the Holy Spirit. I'm grateful He is living within me. I'll never be the same because of the Holy Spirit dwelling in me.

"In Jesus' name. Amen."

Man's Authority in Prayer

We have seen that God has given us His armor and His weapons to wage spiritual warfare. Why has He done this? So that we can win!

Included in this armament is the authority the body of Christ has. When you know *why* you have authority over Satan, you will be confident to *use* that authority. It covers the whole rank and file of Satan's operation from the lowest principalities to the highest wicked spirits in heavenly places. Not one area of human existence is left uncovered by the blood of Jesus. Here is why.

God gave the earth to man. He made Adam in His image and gave him dominion (Gen. 1:28). God said, *Be fruitful, and multiply, and replenish the earth, and subdue it: and have dominion....* Adam was God's under ruler with authority over all of creation. In reflecting this awesome reality, the Psalmist David wrote:

What is man, that thou art mindful of him? and the son of man, that thou visitest him?

For thou hast made him a little lower than the angels, (Hebrew word for angels is *elohiym,* meaning God— Adam was made in the exact likeness of God) *and hast crowned him with glory and honour.*

Thou madest him to have dominion over the works of thy hands: thou hast put all things under his feet. God gave man His Word and His authority. Adam was a free moral agent who determined his own destiny. Adam chose to disobey God's Word. He committed high treason and turned his authority over to Satan. He willfully bowed his knee to a fallen angel. God was obligated to His own Word to Adam. He had to honor his choice. Against God's will, Satan became the god of this world (2 Cor. 4:4).

Adam made his choice. The consequences of it affected the entire human race. Man lost the life and nature of God. He lost his authority over Satan. The nature of spiritual death was lodged in his spirit (Rom. 5:12).

The nature of Satan had passed on to every member of the human race since Adam. Satan became the illegitimate stepfather of mankind. Man was no longer in the family of God.

To redeem mankind, God had to destroy the union between man and the devil. In Genesis 3:15, God prophesied the coming of a Messiah Who would annihilate him. Jesus came to the earth for one reason: to destroy the works of the devil and recapture man's authority (1 John 3:8).

Before the Redeemer came, God dealt with man through the Abrahamic covenant. This contract enabled Abraham and his descendants to live in the blessings until Jesus, *the spotless Son of God* poured out His blood (Gen. 17; Gal. 3:16,17). (Without the shedding of blood there is no remission of sin.) Abraham's responsibility was to live perfect and upright before God. He was not able to do so because of spiritual death. God made provision for his failures with the blood of bulls and goats. The blood of these old covenant sacrifices only *covered* sin (Read Heb. 9 and 10). It could not do away with the sin nature.

The Word that God had spoken (Gen. 3:15) became flesh and dwelt among men (John 1:14). Jesus was born of a virgin. God was His Father giving Him the nature of God in His Spirit. Jesus fulfilled the Abrahamic covenant. He walked perfect and upright in the sight of God as a *man*. Man was the key figure in the Fall and man had to be the key to redemption. Jesus passed the test that Adam failed!

Second Corinthians 5:21 says, *For He* (God) *hath made him* (Jesus) *to be sin for us, who knew no sin; that we might be made the righteousness of God in him.* Jesus *never* committed sin. He *became* sin *for* us.

Since Jesus was *made to be* our sin, He had to pay the penalty for sin. He had to die spiritually and physically, which took Him into the regions of the damned. He went in our place. In Isaiah 53 you find that it pleased God to lay upon Him all of *our* punishment—sin, sickness, poverty, the entire curse (Deut. 28:16-68).

The Cross was a mystery to Satan. The Word tells us that if he had known what was happening, he would not have crucified the Lord of glory (1 Cor. 2:7,8).

Jesus went into hell to free mankind from the penalty of Adam's high treason. Isaiah 53:9 says, *And he made his grave with the wicked, and with the rich in his death...* The Hebrew word for "death" is literally plural. Jesus died two deaths. He died physically and spiritually. When He was made to be sin, He was separated from God. Thus He cried with a loud voice while hanging on the cross, *My God, My God, why hast thou forsaken me?*

Jesus fulfilled the Abrahamic covenant. He bore our disobedience and became the last sacrifice to be offered. His blood did not merely cover sin. It did away with the handwriting of the ordinances that were against us (Col. 2:14). Jesus spent three horrible days and nights in the bowels of this earth repurchasing man's rights and authority by paying the price for man's sin. He took our place...

For as Jonas was three days and three nights in the whale's belly; so shall the Son of man be three days and three nights in the heart of the earth (Matt. 12:40).

Now that he ascended, what is it but that he also descended first into the lower parts of the earth? (Eph. 4:9).

And having spoiled principalities and powers, he made a shew of them openly, triumphing over them in it (Col 2:15). Jesus defeated Satan and his cohorts in his own domain!

God quickened Him with eternal life. *Therefore we are buried with him by baptism into death: that like as Christ was raised up from the dead by the glory of the Father, even so we also should walk in newness of life* (Rom. 6:4). **The power in that life catapulted Him through three realms!** *Wherefore God also hath highly exalted him, and given him a name which is above every name: That at the name of Jesus every knee should bow, of things in heaven, and things in earth, and things under the earth* (Phil. 2:9,10). Nothing could stop the plan of redemption.

In Acts, chapter two, Peter preached how Jesus' soul was not left in hell. He said that David saw the plan of redemption beforehand and spoke of His resurrection (Acts 2:31). The pains of death could not hold Him! He had paid the price for sin.

Hebrews 1:6,8 says, *And AGAIN, when he bringeth in the firstbegotten into the world, he saith, And let all the angels of God worship him. ...Thy throne, O God, is for ever and ever: a sceptre of righteousness is the sceptre of thy kingdom.* Jesus was the firstborn from the dead (Col. 1:18). He took on Himself the nature of sin, paid the price and was reborn into Sonship!

Jesus identified with the human race and became our total substitute. He paid an awesome price for our redemption. When we identify with His death, burial and resurrection, we become born-again sons of God.

That if thou shalt confess with thy mouth the Lord Jesus, and shalt believe in thine heart that God hath raised him from the dead, thou shalt be saved. For with the heart man believeth unto righteousness; and with the mouth confession is made unto salvation (Rom. 10:9,10).

But God, who is rich in mercy, for his great love wherewith he loved us, Even when we were dead in sins, hath quickened us together with Christ, (by grace ye are saved;) And hath raised us up together, and made us sit together in heavenly places in Christ Jesus: That in the ages to come he might shew the exceeding riches of his grace in his kindness toward us through Christ Jesus (Eph. 2:4-7).

Jesus is now seated at the right hand of the Father expecting His enemies to be made His footstool. Jesus is the Head and we are His body. The feet are in the body. He is expecting *His* enemies to be put under *our* feet.

Authority over the devil has been given into the hands of the body of Christ. That authority carries command in the world of the spirit. It is backed by the whole plan of redemption!

The things that we have studied are things that you must accept by faith in God's Word. You cannot see them with your natural eyes. Nevertheless, they are realities in the spirit.

Put yourself in Satan's position and see this from his viewpoint. If you were Satan, what would you think? Standing before you is a soldier, clad in a complete set of God's armor—the breastplate of righteousness, the helmet of salvation, the girdle of truth, the shoes of the Gospel of peace, the shield of faith, and the sword of the Spirit. This soldier is speaking God's Word with authority. With the face mask pulled down, you could not tell the difference between him and Jesus. If you were Satan, wouldn't you give careful consideration before you jumped into combat with him? This same image has already eternally wounded him in defeat once. Satan says, "Once is enough, I'll flee!"

The only way a believer will tip off Satan is by lifting his faceplate through unbelief. As long as he acts and lives by faith, Satan will be unable to defeat him. The

Wuest translation of James 4:7,8 says, "Be subject with implicit obedience to God at once and once for all. Stand immovable against the onset of the devil and he will flee from you. Draw near to God and He will draw near to you."

You have been given the whole armor of God. Your responsibility is to pick it up, put it on, and wear it in faith. You have the Holy Spirit and the Word of God. You have the authority in the realm of the spirit. **You have been fully equipped with weapons that guarantee results in prayer.** You can expect results *every* time you pray!

Chapter IV
Prayer That Changes Things

The following types of prayers are means by which you can change things:

The prayer of agreement, (2)of binding and (3)loosing, of (4)petition and supplication, (5)intercession, and (6)united prayer.

Always remember that prayer changes *things;* it does not change God. One of the mighty attributes of God is that He is the same yesterday, today and forever (Heb. 13:8). **What you want to do is take your faith and the Word of God and change the circumstances in your life to line up with His will.** His plans and desires are always for *your* success and well-being.

Some people think that if they pray long and hard they will get God to do something for them. The Word says that God's eyes are over the righteous and His ears are open to their prayers (Ps. 34:15). If you have made Jesus the Lord of your life, you are *the righteousness* of God in Christ Jesus. He is already open to your prayers. Through prayer, you tap into *His* strength and change the things that are out of line with His will.

The Prayer of Agreement

When used according to God's Word, the prayer of agreement will cover every circumstance in life.

The foundation scripture for the prayer of agreement is Matthew 18:18-20: *Verily I say unto you, Whatsoever ye shall bind on earth shall be bound in heaven: and whatsoever ye shall loose on earth shall be loosed in heaven. Again I say unto you, That if two of you shall agree on earth as touching any thing that they shall ask, it shall be done for them of my Father which is in heaven. For where two or three are gathered together in my name, there am I in the midst of them.*

Let me use finances to illustrate. The **first** thing to do is agree with God's Word. Read the scriptures and pray. Gloria and I sometimes write down our agreement like this: "We hereby agree, according to Philippians 4:19 and Matthew 18:19 as follows: 'Father, we see in Your Word that You will supply all of our needs according to Your riches in glory. We are setting ourselves in agreement that our financial need is met according to Your Word. We believe we receive (Be specific)_____ _____. We establish this agreement, in Jesus' name. Amen.'"

Amen means *"So be it."* As far as we are concerned, the matter is closed. We just thank God from that point forward. We know that if we want results WE MUST NOT WAVER. To waver is to doubt.

If Satan brings doubts, we simply speak to him in the authority of Jesus' name and say, "Don't bring us your lies. Not only is it written in God's Word, but we have agreed. We have written it down." As far as we are concerned, the need is met. There is no doubt about it because we have agreed according to the Word of God. Consequently, our confession and actions will be in line with what we have established as truth.

(Of course, there have been times when we have wavered. Then we must take it to God and receive forgiveness for unbelief, reinforce our original decree and go again. We all make mistakes in the walk of faith. The important thing is to keep walking. If you miss, go again. The biggest mistake of all is to get discouraged and quit before you receive your answer.)

I challenge you to write down your agreements. Seeing

40

it in black and white on paper will make a difference! You will be more likely to line up your confession and your actions with your agreement.

Jesus said that if any two on earth agree, He would be in the midst of that agreement to see that it comes to pass. You are on earth so you qualify. If you agree with another believer as touching *anything* that lines up with the Word of God, He is there in your midst to carry it out.

Jesus wants you to agree. He will see to it that it comes to pass. The word "agree" is translated in the Amplified Bible as "agree and harmonize together or make a symphony together." The word "symphony" caught my ear one time so I looked it up and found that it means "all available instruments in harmony." You must have your spirit, your mind, and your actions in agreement with the Word.

Agreeing spiritually is to agree on the Word of God. Make up your mind that God's Word is true and that it *will* come to pass.

Secondly, be strong in your mind. That is Satan's battleground. You must control your thoughts. Writing it down will be beneficial for this reason. It will keep it before your eyes. When your mind tries to change directions, just control it with your agreement on God's Word. Do not tie God's hands. Allow Him to work.

You have agreed spirit and soul (mind). Then your actions must come in line. If finances are what you agreed upon, expect the money to come in. This is part of being in agreement. You can not agree in prayer about something and then act oppositely and expect it to come to pass. If you do, it will eventually take over your thinking.

Agreement with the Word and with another believer are not the only things involved in this type of prayer. Agreement is also harmony.

Harmony is extremely important. When speaking of prayer in Mark 11:25,26, Jesus said, *And when ye stand praying, forgive, if ye have ought against any: that your Father also which is in heaven may forgive you your trespasses. But if ye do not forgive, neither will your Father which is in heaven forgive your trespasses.* This is vital in your prayer life. You *must* forgive everyone who has offended you. He did not say, "think about it for six weeks and then forgive if and when you *feel* better." He said, **FORGIVE WHEN YOU PRAY.**

Jesus prayed, *Our Father which art in heaven, Hallowed be Thy name. Thy kingdom come, Thy will be done in earth, as it is in heaven. Give us this day our daily bread, and forgive us our trespasses as we forgive those who trespass against us.* He put a condition on forgiveness. The condition was "I don't expect to be forgiven *until* and *when* I forgive." He displayed the kind of discipline the believer should exercise when he is praying.

How really important is this? In Galatians 5:6, the Bible says that faith works by love. If you are operating with an unforgiving heart, your prayer life is paralyzed.

The Word says that we know we have the petitions we have desired of Him *if* we do the things that are pleasing in His sight. Put these scriptures together and you quickly see that unforgiveness would actually ruin the whole prayer system.

Agreement makes prayer work. You can experience a place of agreement with God's Word and harmony that will produce power as you forgive and as you agree with another believer. You can affect governments, families and the lives of others. You can change your financial situation, affect your church, your pastor, etc. with the power of prayer. Find someone who can agree with you according to the Word of God.

The same principle works the other way. If you are in disagreement, the door is open for Satan to come in. *For where envying and strife is, there is confusion and every evil work* (James 3:16).

In the 18th chapter of Matthew, Peter came up to Jesus and said, "How many times should I forgive my brother, seven times?" Jesus said, "...until seventy times seven." **Forgive because God said to and not because you feel like it.**

Build your home, your church, etc. on the unselfish love of God. *Selfishness has never built anything that it did not destroy as well.* Love never fails. The love of God is the very center of the family of God because God is love. You are His very own child. You are born-again with His love nature. Don't let that love lie dormant. Cast down selfishness and let loose the love of God that is in you. You cannot fail when love is in dominion.

When you forgive and reach for harmony, you come to the place where you have the spiritual awareness to perceive the closeness of God. Jesus said that if you get into harmony and agree together, that He would be *in the midst* of you. You are praying with a God that is involved.

When you are in harmony and agreement with those around you, you will step into a deeper, more personal fellowship with God. He becomes real and vital to you. **Fellowship with your heavenly Father is one of the greatest things you will ever have in your Christian walk!** It causes a confidence and an assurance deep down in your heart. You know that your prayers are answered because you have conformed yourself to His will. As you forgive, the joy that comes through answered prayer will become your own personal experience. Jesus said, *Ask, and ye shall receive, that your joy may be full* (John 16:24).

The Prayer of Binding and Loosing

God intends for the body of Christ to police the evil

forces of this world. We are to change circumstances to line up with God's will and put Satan under our feet through the power of God. We are to spoil his plans, plots and maneuvers against God's people!

The prayer of binding and loosing puts a halt to Satan's activities. Matthew 12:29 says, *Or else how can one enter into a strong man's house, and spoil his goods, except he first bind the strong man? and then he will spoil his house.* You have authority over Satan (Luke 10:19). You exercise it with the prayer of binding and loosing. *Verily I say unto you, Whatsoever ye shall bind on earth shall be bound in heaven: and whatsoever ye shall loose on earth shall be loosed in heaven* (Matt. 18:18).

As you enforce the authority vested in the church, speak directly to Satan. Exercise your faith in the work of Jesus at Calvary.

When Jesus was raised from the dead, He stripped Satan of his authority over mankind. That authority has been delegated to the body of Christ in the earth. Bind Satan in the name of Jesus.

Many times Gloria and I add a paragraph to our agreement prayer: "Satan, we bind you and render you helpless in this situation. As a matter of record, you are hereby bound in the name of Jesus." From then on, we thank God that Satan is bound and unable to work in the situation. We refuse to give him any place.

The ultimate choice is yours whether or not to receive from God. Jesus asked the man at the pool of Bethesda, "Wilt thou be made whole?" In other words, "Do you want to stay the way you are, or do you want to be made whole?" His attitude is still the same. The choice is yours. God has already provided the way out for you.

Do not give Satan any place by talking about the problem after you have agreed and bound him. Instead of talking the problem, talk the answer—God's Word.

Loose the angelic forces of God to see that it comes to pass. Hebrews 1:13,14 describes the angels as ministering spirits, sent to minister for them who shall be heirs of salvation. They minister *for* us. In other words, they are messengers sent to work in our behalf. Say: "Ministering spirits, I loose you in the name of Jesus, to minister in my behalf according to the will of God."

The Prayer of Petition and Supplication

The words *petition* and *supplication* are defined as "a formal request of a higher power." This prayer changes things. It is based on Philippians 4:6, *Be careful for nothing; but in every thing by prayer and supplication with thanksgiving let your requests be made known unto God.*

To illustrate, suppose you obtained an audience with the governor of your state. After you went through the proper channels, would you then enter his office without being prepared? Of course not! You would have your ideas formulated and the arguments settled in your mind long before you obtained an audience with him. Shouldn't you handle yourself in the same way when approaching God? Hebrews 4:16 says, *Let us therefore come boldly unto the throne of grace....*

Do not go into the prayer of petition and supplication without knowing what you want to say and how you want to say it. Enter the throne room with your petition drawn up according to God's Word. Ask yourself these questions: What happened at Calvary? How did the substitutionary sacrifice of Jesus affect this trial I am facing? Then, find out what God has already done regarding your situation. If you need healing, look up those scriptures pertaining to healing. Present your petition. No matter what your situation may be, God has provided an answer for it in His Word. The Cross paid the price for your deliverance.

United Prayer

So when they had further threatened them, they let them go, finding nothing how they might punish them, because of the people: for all men glorified God for that which was done.

For the man was above forty years old, on whom this miracle of healing was shewed.

And being let go, they went to their own company, and reported all that the chief priests and elders had said unto them.

And when they heard that, they lifted up their voice to God with one accord, and said, Lord, thou art God, which hast made heaven, and earth, and the sea, and all that in them is:

Who by the mouth of thy servant David hast said, Why did the heathen rage, and the people imagine vain things?

The kings of the earth stood up, and the rulers were gathered together against the Lord, and against his Christ.

For of a truth against thy holy child Jesus, whom thou hast anointed, both Herod, and Pontius Pilate, with the Gentiles, and the people of Israel, were gathered together,

For to do whatsoever thy hand and thy counsel determined before to be done.

And now, Lord, behold their threatenings: and grant unto thy servants, that with all boldness they may speak thy word,

By stretching forth thine hand to heal; and that signs and wonders may be done by the name of thy holy child Jesus.

And when they had prayed, the place was shaken where they were assembled together; and they were all filled with the Holy Ghost, and they spake the word of God with boldness.

Acts 4:21-31

In this day and time, united prayer is seldomly discussed. In most of the instances in the Bible where there is a body of believers, we find that they pray in a united manner. However, in many of our churches today, somebody usually *leads* in prayer. Very little is taught from the Word about praying together out loud at one time.

The previous scripture is the basis for united prayer. Peter and John had been arrested and appeared before the religious council. Their lives were threatened if they continued to preach in the name of Jesus. They went back to their own company and told everyone what had happened. When they heard, they all prayed. **An absolutely tremendous amount of power is involved in united prayer.**

What were the results of this prayer? Acts 5:12 says, *And by the hands of the apostles were many signs and wonders wrought among the people.* Their one request was answered exactly the way they prayed it. The political system of the day tried but **they could not stop the power of God in operation.** This united prayer was offered accurately according to the Word of God.

As a body of believers, we need to get in one accord on the Word of God and expect results. It will cause things to change!

Chapter V
Intercessory Prayer

The prayer of intercession is prayed in behalf of others. Through His Word, God has called the body of Christ to the ministry of intercession. *I exhort therefore, that, first of all, supplications, prayers, intercessions, and giving of thanks, be made for all men; For kings, and for all that are in authority; that we may lead a quiet and peaceable life in all godliness and honesty. For this is good and acceptable in the sight of God our Saviour; Who will have all men to be saved, and to come unto the knowledge of the truth* (1 Tim. 2:1-4).

Very recently, during a time of fasting, God revealed to me that He is calling the church to rally around the prayer of intercession. We are to call on Him to pour out of His Spirit in these last days in great, unusual manifestations of His power. God is about to bring forth the grand finale. It will be the greatest production by the Spirit of God in the history of the human race.

We are the most privileged generation to have ever lived on this earth. We are blessed not only to witness these manifestations, but also to be the vessels through which His mighty power will flow.

The miraculous things that occurred in the early church as recorded in the Book of Acts will be common among us in these last days. **Intercessory prayer is the tool that the Spirit of God will use to bring them into manifestation.**

We are entering into the most exciting move of the Holy Spirit that the church has ever experienced. I believe that this is the last big thrust to harvest the souls of this world into the kingdom of God.

Why are we called to intercession? Because God does not do anything in the earth without the cooperation of a man. He intends that we work *together* with Him to accomplish His will. Man still is in authority in the earth. God put him in that position by His will.

I believe that we are the generation that will usher in the coming of the Lord Jesus Christ for His church. Before He comes, the Spirit of God will be poured out upon **all** flesh.

Behold, the husbandman waiteth for the precious fruit of the earth, and hath long patience for it, until he receive the early and the latter rain (James 5:7). John, the 15th chapter tells us that the husbandman is the heavenly Father. The fruit of the earth is the harvest of souls. The rain is the outpouring of the Holy Spirit (Hos. 6:3).

Intercessory prayer causes the rain of God's Spirit to bring the harvest of the human race into the family of God. Right now, all over this world, God is bringing the body of Christ into unity. As rivers of living water, the believers that are joined together will cause a flood of God's power in the earth.

Because of the crucial time that we are living in, this move of the Holy Spirit is causing believers everywhere to respond to the call to intercession. **This world will not take much more sin!** Romans 8:22 says that all of creation *groans* for the manifestation of the sons of God. Heaven is reverberating twenty-four hours a day with the intercession of God's people.

We are at the end of what began on the day of Pentecost. The Apostle Peter said:

But this is that which was spoken by the prophet Joel; And it shall come to pass in the last days, saith God, I will pour out

*of my Spirit upon all flesh: and your sons and your daughters
shall prophesy, and your young men shall see visions, and
your old men shall dreams dreams: And on my servants and
on my handmaidens I will pour out in those days of my Spirit;
and they shall prophesy: And I will show wonders in heaven
above, and signs in the earth beneath* (Acts 2:16-19). The
result of this outpouring of the Holy Spirit is:

*And it shall come to pass, that whosoever shall call on the
name of the Lord shall be saved* (verse 21).

In order to be saved, one must be born into the family
of God. Jesus said, *Except a man be born again, he cannot
see the kingdom of God* (John 3:3). He was speaking of the
spiritual new birth. *That which is born of flesh is flesh; and
that which is born of the Spirit is spirit* (verses 5 and 6).
Intercession is giving birth in the realm of the spirit.

Did you notice the words *servants* and *handmaidens* in
Acts 2:18? When you are born again, you do not become
a servant of God. You become a child of God. In order
to become a servant or handmaiden, you must make a
choice. W. E. Vine says these words mean "one who
gives himself up to the will of another." Because of your
love for God, you choose to *serve Him*. You yield your
will to His will and become a co-laborer with Him.
**Those who totally give themselves to His service will
be God's mouthpiece in the earth. They will be the
vehicles of His Spirit.**

The Apostle Paul called himself a servant of Jesus
Christ. W. E. Vine's Expository Dictionary defines
"servant" as being in "subjection without the idea of
bondage; the perfect example being Christ Himself."
Paul had the right to go free, but didn't. He served his
Master out of love and dedication. God is calling us to
be *the Master's* servants. Jesus said that many are called
but few are chosen (Matt. 20:16). In other words, few
dedicate themselves to servitude. Upon those and out of

those who are dedicated to Him, God will pour out of His Spirit upon all flesh.

Jesus said, ...*whosoever drinketh of the water that I shall give him shall never thirst; but the water that I shall give him shall be in him a well of water springing up into everlasting life* (John 4:14). The Spirit of God is a well of living water **inside of you,** springing up. A well is for personal use. God's ultimate purpose is that other thirsty souls can partake of that water. He desires to pour out of His Spirit from the inside of *you* through intercession. *He that believeth on me, as the scripture hath said, out of his belly shall flow rivers of living water* (John 7:38). A river is for everyone's use. The outpouring of the Spirit is a flow of the Holy Spirit coming from inside the believer. That flow is the source of all the signs and wonders and miracles! *Everyone,* the scripture says *all flesh,* will benefit. Intercessory prayer is going to play *the* major role in this outpouring. It is what causes God's power to flow in the earth unhindered.

Prayer is the doorway into the mightiest release of power that is known to man. It brings the very presence of God to and upon man in any part of the world. That power operates as believers allow those rivers of living water to gush toward the dry and thirsty. The torrential outpouring of the Spirit will cause life to spring forth in those who receive the seed of God's Word. The result is the harvest of new creatures in Christ Jesus (1 Pet. 1:23).

Let's study the art of intercession. Isaiah 59:16,17 says, *And he saw that there was no man, and wondered that there was no intercessor: therefore his arm brought salvation unto him; and his righteousness, it sustained him. For he put on righteousness as a breastplate, and an helmet of salvation upon his head; and he put on the garments of vengeance for clothing, and was clad with zeal as a cloak.* What is His arm? **Jesus.** The sole purpose Jesus came to the earth was to be that intercessor. He wore the helmet of salvation and the breastplate of righteousness. That is the same armor in the sixth chapter of Ephesians for the body of Christ. Jesus came as an intercessor. *We* are to put on that same armor and enter into the same field of prayer. His arm is bringing salvation again. As intercessors, we are His arm in the earth causing reconciliation between men and God. Jesus said, *As my Father hath sent me, even so send I you* (John 20:21). The armor is the same and the calling is the same.

You may say, "Do you mean to tell me that I have the same calling on my life that Jesus had?" **Absolutely!** Second Corinthians 5:18 says that we have been given the ministry of reconciliation. Jesus said, "*You* go into all the world, and *you* preach the Gospel to every creature." He also said, "The works that I do shall you do also; and greater than these shall you do; because I go unto my Father" (John 14:12). He went didn't He? Then, you and I are responsible for the works. He provided us with the new birth. God said in Ezekiel 36:26 that a new spirit He would put within us. *And* that He would put His spirit in us. That gives us the right and the miraculous power to enter into the intercessory prayer ministry.

Intercession is the highest expression of love. It is loving in the spirit, applying spiritual power for another person. It will overpower the evil influences that have bound that person. Your prayer may be for salvation, healing, or any other area of deliverance from Satan.

Second Corinthians 4:3,4 says: *But if our gospel be hid, it is hid to them that are lost: In whom the god of this world hath blinded the minds of them which believe not, lest the light of the glorious gospel of Christ, who is the image of God should shine unto them.*

Satan has blinded the minds of those who have not received the Gospel. Your intercessory prayer wrestles against evil spirits that have deceived them. It is literally giving yourself, your time, your life for others. Jesus said, *Greater love hath no man than this, that a man lay down his life for his friends.* This is the God kind of love. It is unselfish. The world did not know this kind of love until Jesus came to the earth. He laid down His life to come to earth and live as a man. He emptied Himself of His divine privileges and fulfilled His earthly ministry as a *man,* filled with the Holy Spirit. *But made himself of no reputation, and took upon him the form of a servant, and was made in the likeness of men: And being found in fashion as a man, he humbled himself, and became obedient unto death, even the death of the cross* (Phil. 2:7,8). Love motivated God to send Him. *For God so loved the world, that he gave his only begotten Son, that whosoever believeth in him should not perish, but have everlasting life* (John 3:16). Jesus' love for the Father impelled Him to obey. He said, *My meat is to do the will of him that sent me, and to finish his work* (John 4:34).

Jesus has provided reconciliation between God and man through His substitutionary sacrifice at Calvary. **We are co-laborers with Him.** Redemption was bought with a high price. Jesus didn't take it lightly and neither should we. God's heart was hungry for a family. Jesus freely gave Himself for this desire. What an act of love!

God's heart is still hungry. He yearns to have *every* sinner restored unto Himself through the new birth and every believer in close fellowship with Him.

To give your life means to give everything. Jesus came as an Intercessor. He is still giving Himself today. Hebrews 7:25 says,*He ever liveth to make intercession.* We have said, "Jesus gave His life for us." But, no, He is *giving* His life for us. He is still interceding. His body in the earth is wearing the same prayer armor He wore. We have inherited His armor to do His work and enter into His ministry of intercession.

We have been given that same love that motivated Jesus to come as *the* Intercessor! Romans 5:5 says that the love of God has been shed abroad in our hearts by the

Holy Spirit. **The love that desires to lay down its own desires and to intercede for someone else is abiding on the inside of us!** The love that impelled Jesus to go to the cross compels us to intercede. We pray for others so that they can come to the knowledge of the truth.

Through the knowledge of God's Word, we realize that we also have His love that urges us to reach out toward others. It urges us to be soul-winners. A soul-winner is an intercessor in action. Jesus paid the price and is paying the price to win souls. Intercessory prayer softens their hearts to receive the message of the Gospel.

When you are filled with the Holy Spirit, you receive the ability to speak in another language. *And they were all filled with the Holy Ghost, and began to speak with other tongues, as the Spirit gave them utterance* (Acts 2:4). The Holy Spirit gives the utterance and you do the speaking.

Just as English is the voice of your mind, praying in tongues is the voice of your spirit. It is your spirit speaking mysteries unto God (1 Cor. 14:2). The Apostle Paul said, *If I pray in an unknown tongue, my spirit prayeth, but my understanding is unfruitful* (1 Cor. 14:14).

The Holy Spirit knows what is needed in the lives of others when you do not know (Rom. 8:26). **Praying in other tongues is the most valuable tool that you have in intercessory prayer.** When you pray in other tongues, you operate in the realm of the spirit. The weapons of your warfare are **mighty** through God to the pulling down of strongholds.

When you move in this area of intercession, your physical man will be your spirit man's assistant. You begin to speak in a language that comes out of the inner man. The Spirit of the Living God can speak to your own human spirit. Out of it will come rivers of living water. You are not just praying mentally limited prayers. When you pray in tongues, you pray beyond your own limited knowledge. You have moved beyond the natural into the spirit. You have to yield to it as an act of your will.

If you are not filled with the Spirit, ask God to fill you right *now*. Put down this book, ask the Lord to fill you with His Spirit, and then open your mouth and allow your new prayer language to flow.

Your first prayer assignment is not for yourself. It is to pray for all men; for kings and men in high authority (1 Tim. 2:1-4). When you respond to the call of intercession, the Holy Spirit prays the perfect will of God through you.

Begin praying for a given body of people: A family, a village, a country, a state, or a nation. You do not need to wait for a burden for this. The Word says that Jesus was moved with compassion (Matt. 9:36). **Compassion is not a feeling, it is a person.** Separate yourself from the things of this world. Get in your prayer closet alone with God and **commit** to intercession. *Yield* to the love of God inside you. All the motivation you need will come that way. The One who *ever liveth to make intercession* is living in you! He's already motivated! Yield to Him.

Isaiah 64:7 says, *And there is none that calleth upon thy name, that stirreth up himself to take hold of thee....* The Spirit of God will not be able to help you intercede unless you are willing to stir yourself and take that position of intercession. Paul told Timothy to stir up the gift that was in him (2 Tim. 1:6). *You* stir it up!

Begin to pray by making yourself available to the Holy Spirit. Yield! Allow Him to use you to pray for the man who does not have anybody to pray for him. Stand in the gap for him. Start where you are and allow it to spread to the world. You are literally fighting spiritual warfare in their behalf. The Apostle Paul said, *For I would that ye knew what great conflict I have for you, and for them at Laodicea, and for as many as have not seen my face in the flesh* (Col. 2:1). This was the same conflict that Paul

56

talked about in the sixth chapter of Ephesians, when he said that we wrestle against principalities, powers, rulers of the darkness of this world, and wicked spirits in heavenly places (Eph. 6:12). The family of God is not based on selfishness. It is based on love. Intercession is the highest expression of love.

When you commit yourself to pray for those who need Jesus, remember that the Bible says you are going to have to bind Satan in order to spoil his house (Matt. 12:29). You are confronting all the forces of evil that have them bound. Do not stop just because it looks like they will never receive. Your intercession is placing pressure on Satan and his forces. Do not relent but persevere in prayer. It is up to that person to make his own choice.

Through your intercession, they will be able to make it. They will no longer be blinded by Satan.

Take these scriptures before the Holy Spirit and give Him the opportunity to reveal them to you personally. He is the Teacher. He can show you how they work. You can stir up the gift within you simply by *desiring* to know how intercession works.

Before spiritual births take place, travail goes forth. In the natural realm, a woman does not give birth without labor. In the spirit, travail is the labor that brings forth the new birth. Intercession is God's heartbeat because it is the labor that births the souls of this world into His family.

We noticed in Isaiah 64:7 it spoke of stirring oneself up. Isaiah 66:8 says, *Who hath heard such a thing? who hath seen such things? Shall the earth be made to bring forth in one day? or shall a nation be born at once? for as soon as Zion travailed, she brought forth her children.* Let's find out who Zion is and what she does to travail, and how the children are brought in.

Hebrews 12:22,23 says, *But ye are come unto mount Sion, and unto the city of the living God, the heavenly*

Jerusalem, and to an innumerable company of angels, To the general assembly and church of the firstborn, which are written in heaven, and to God the Judge of all, and to the spirits of just men made perfect.... Zion is the church of the firstborn. Jesus is the firstborn of many brethren (Rom. 8:29). Zion is the church of Jesus Christ. If you are a member of the body of Christ, you are Zion.

In Galatians 4:19 Paul said, *My little children, of whom I travail in birth again....* If he is going to travail again, he had to have once travailed in order to bring the little children to birth.

Travail causes others to be born again. Why would it say "birth?" Why would it say "travail?" Why would it compare to birth? Jesus said out of the *belly*, the deepest interior of a man, would flow these rivers of living water (John 7:38). Stir yourself up and start praying in other tongues. Your spirit is praying. Keep at it. Soon you will notice that the Holy Spirit will take hold together with you. You will begin to travail as if in labor.

You may groan out loud. You are releasing spiritual power. The Word says that the *effectual, fervent* prayer of a righteous man availeth much (James 5:16). The Amplified translation says that the effectual, fervent heartfelt prayer of a righteous man makes much power available. This is the art of intercession. It is stirring yourself up to take hold with the Holy Spirit to cause eternal changes in the lives of others.

Romans 8:26 says, *Likewise the Spirit also helpeth our infirmities.* The word "helpeth" is translated in the Greek from three words which mean "takes hold together with us against." That verse literally reads: *Likewise the Spirit also **takes hold together with us against** our infirmities: for we know not what we should pray for as we ought: but the Spirit itself maketh intercession for us with groanings which cannot be uttered. And he that searcheth the hearts knoweth what is the mind of the Spirit, because he* *maketh intercession for the saints according to the will of God.* He is telling the body of Christ about the forces that are available through intercession. The Holy Spirit sees to it that God's will is carried out even in areas where we do not know how to pray. He searches the heart and He knows the mind of the spirit of a man. In other words, *you can go beyond your own mental ability and knowledge.*

God's purpose is for us to begin to pray for one another. Intercession gives the Holy Spirit the opportunity to bring the fullness of God's will to pass in the earth.

Chapter VI
Kinds of Prayer

Stand therefore...Praying always with all prayer and supplication in the Spirit (Eph. 6:14,18).

God's Word instructs us to *pray always with all prayer.* Other translations say, *all kinds of prayer* or *different kinds of prayer.* The *Amplified Bible* says, *with all manner of prayer.* **There is more than just one kind of prayer,** depending on what you desire from the Lord. Let's discuss each one in the light of God's Word.

Prayer of Dedication and Worship

> *Then cometh Jesus with them unto a place called Gethsemane, and saith unto the disciples, Sit ye here, while I go and pray yonder. And he took with him Peter and the two sons of Zebedee, and began to be sorrowful and very heavy. Then saith he unto them, My soul is exceeding sorrowful, even unto death: tarry ye here, and watch with me. And he went a little farther, and fell on his face, and prayed, saying, O my Father, if it be possible, let this cup pass from me: nevertheless not as I will, but as thou wilt.*
>
> Matthew 26:36-39.

The prayer of dedication and worship holds a tremendous amount of power. We need to know how it works and when it is to be used. In the past, it has been misunderstood. When the leper came up to Him and said, "I know you can make me well if you will," Jesus said, "I will." He already knew God's will was healing. He did not have to pray, "If it be Thy will." God's will is to be done on earth as it is in heaven (Matt. 6:9,10). Heaven has no sickness.

The only prayer in which you can pray the word "if" and it not be unbelief is dedication and worship. The word "if" can create unbelief. Praying for healing, whether it be yours or someone elses, is a prayer that changes things.

Unbelief does not make prayer work. Most people pray, "if it be Thy will," thinking they are being humble. Actually, they are ignorant of the Word of God. Unbelief will not bring results.

The prayer of dedication is getting your will in line with God's will to bring success into the situation. God's will is always to your advantage. Proverbs 16:3 in the Amplified translation says, *Roll your works upon the Lord—commit and trust them wholly to Him; [He will cause your thoughts to become agreeable to His will, and] so shall your plans be established and succeed.*

The prayer of dedication puts you and God aiming toward the same goal. So many times people are running in the opposite direction, hoping God is going to support their endeavors. You should get God involved with those endeavors before you ever move! **Never be afraid to yield your will to God; He wants you to succeed!**

When you pray the prayer of dedication, and live by it, you will experience the peace of God because you are truly trusting Him. Isaiah 26:3 says, *Thou wilt keep him in perfect peace, whose mind is stayed on thee: because he trusteth in thee.*

Thanksgiving and Praise

The Bible says that if you pray according to God's will, you know that He hears you and that you have the petitions that you desired of Him (1 John 5:14,15). God's Word is His will.

God is faithful. His Word can be relied upon. Do not wait until you can see the manifestation before you believe you have it. That will put you over into an area of waiting and hoping. If you believe you receive *when you pray*, begin to praise God for the answer.

Faith involves thanksgiving and praise. Philippians 4:6 says, "Be careful for nothing; but in every thing let your requests be made known unto God with thanksgiving." The thanksgiving and the praise are integral parts of the prayer.

You and God are working together. It is your prayer and His power.

Praise is more than just words. There is power in praise. God did not ordain praise just so that we could brag on Him. Psalm eight says, *O Lord our Lord, how excellent is thy name in all the earth! who hast set thy glory above the heavens. Out of the mouth of babes and sucklings hast thou ordained strength because of thine enemies, that thou mightest still the enemy and the avenger.* Jesus quoted this verse of scripture and said, *Out of the mouth of babes and sucklings thou hast perfected praise* (Matt. 21:16). Strength and praise are one and the same according to the Word of God. **God ordained praise to stop Satan in his tracks.**

Once you have believed that you received because of the Word, your faith is in action. Through praise you are throwing your faith up against that mountain of adversity in your life. Jesus said that if you have faith and doubt not, you can speak to the mountain and it will be removed. You will have what you say. If you quit applying the force of faith, the mountain will not be removed. You want the mountain to keep moving until it sinks into the sea and is completely out of sight! **Apply the force of faith by praising God that it is gone!**

The only way Satan can stop you and your faith is with unbelief. He does not have any power to stop God. He cannot stop that mountain from moving into the sea. The only way he can succeed is to make you quit applying the pressure.

The mountain may be sickness, disease, alcohol, family trouble, financial trouble, or any evil work. Jesus bought and paid for the answer to all of it. You cannot face any problem that has not been taken care of through Calvary's cross.

The psalmist David said, *I will praise thee, O Lord, with my whole heart; I will shew forth all thy marvellous works. I will be glad and rejoice in thee: I will sing praise to thy name, O thou most High. When mine enemies are turned back, they shall fall and perish at thy presence.* He did not say *if.* He said *when* the enemies fall back! As you praise God, those enemies will retreat. The Bible says that He inhabits the praises of His people (Ps. 22:3).

Praise is not something that you just feel once in a while. God is worthy of your praise. The Bible says to offer the sacrifice of praise. What did they do in the Old Testament when they had problems that they could not overcome? The priest would offer sacrifices to God and bring Him on the scene. God stopped the onslaught of the enemy. As a new covenant believer, you are a priest of God. No other sacrifice can be offered. Jesus offered the ultimate blood sacrifice. As a priest, you offer the sacrifice of praise. Hebrews 13:15 says, *By him therefore let us offer the sacrifice of praise to God continually, that is, the fruit of our lips giving thanks to his name.*

In Luke, 17, beginning with the 11th verse, Jesus ministered to ten men who had leprosy. They said, *Jesus, Master, have mercy on us. And when he saw them, he*

64

said unto them, Go shew yourselves unto the priests. And it came to pass, that, as they went, they were cleansed. The Bible says, *And one of them, when he saw that he was healed, turned back, and with a loud voice glorified (praised) God.* They were all cleansed. But only one praised God unashamedly. Jesus said, ''Were not the other nine cleansed? Where are they?'' Then He said to the man, *Thy faith hath made thee whole.* The others were cleansed but he was *made whole!* His faith kept working. His mountain did not stop at the seashore or sink halfway into the sea! No trace of his mountain was left. Whatever the disease had destroyed was restored.

That is the kind of power that you can have right now in your own life. If you are not familiar with praising God, or it makes you feel uncomfortable, ask God to show you how. You can start by reading the Psalms aloud. They speak of the great and mighty works of God. They praise Him for His power, mercy, etc. God is faithful to perfect your praises!

The Prayer of Committal

If you will practice what I am about to share with you, this will be the last day you will ever have a worried thought. You can commit yourself and all of the cares and worries of your mind to Him and enjoy divine peace.

God is vehemently against worry. It does not produce anything but stress, strain and death. Jesus preached against it; Paul preached against it. The whole Bible is against worry because Satan designed it.

Take Philippians 4:6,7 as a command. *Be careful for nothing; but in every thing by prayer and supplication with thanksgiving let your requests be made known unto God. And the peace of God, which passeth all understanding, shall keep your hearts and minds through Christ Jesus.* The Amplified Bible says, *Do not fret or have any anxiety about anything.* First Peter 5:6,7 says, *Humble yourselves therefore under the mighty hand of God, that he my exalt you in due time. Casting all your care upon him.* Not 75 percent of it. Not everything but your kids. He did not say, "everything but your finances." Your confession every morning should be, **"I do not have a care, because it has been cast over on my Lord."** Cast out every single worried thought that would trample its way into your thinking. Roll it over on to Him.

Let me illustrate how you would do it. Let's say you were standing about 20 feet away from me. I tossed the keys to my automobile to you. If someone else were to come to me and say, "Brother Copeland, I need the keys to your car, I need to use it." I would say, "No, I can't help you. I cast my keys over on him. I don't have them." I did not say that those keys ceased to exist. I did not say that he could not have these keys. I did not say that I could not get them back. If I go and get them, you would give them back to me. If someone wants the car keys they will have to go talk to you because I cast them over on you.

That's what we need to do with our cares. We must cast them over on the Lord and not take them back! If Satan brings a worried thought to your mind, saying, "What if...," then you can tell him to talk to God about it. It is in His hands, not yours!

Many people want God to supernaturally remove their worry. But that is not the way to get the peace of God. It comes by acting on the Word that says to cast all of your worry and anxiety over on Him. You must replace those thoughts with the Word. Philippians 4:8 says to think on whatsoever things that are true, honest, just, pure, lovely, of good report. If there be any virtue, if there be any praise, *think on these things.*

You are the one that has to control your mind. The Word says that the peace of God will garrison and mount guard over your heart and mind (Phil. 4:7, *Amplified Bible*).

You are going to have to do something. You must keep your thoughts under control.

Second Corinthians 10:5 says, *Casting down imaginations, and every high thing that exalteth itself against the knowledge of God, and bringing into captivity every thought to the obedience of Christ.* I have had people tell me that they can't quit worrying. They can! The verse before that says that the weapons of our warfare are not carnal. They are **powerful** through God to the pulling down of strongholds. The strongholds of Satan are in the mind. He makes suggestions like, "it won't work," and "what if," and "but." Anybody can stop worrying!

The power of God begins to operate when you cast your care over on Him. As long as you worry about it, you only hinder the flow of His power and tie His hands.

Take these three scriptures, 1 Peter 5:6,7; 2 Corinthians 10:5, and Philippians 4:6 and meditate them. Joshua 1:8 says that if you will meditate in the Word day and night, you will be able to see how to *do* it. Philipians 4:9 says, *Those things, which ye have both learned, and received, and heard, and seen in me, do.* As you give your attention to these scriptures the Holy Spirit will reveal this truth to you. You will then be able to act on it!

The 13th verse of Philippians 4 is the finale: *I can do all things through Christ which strengtheneth me.* You don't have to worry again. The greater One indwells you. He is able to put you over. Commit to it. You will never worry again.

Chapter VII
Fasting and Prayer

There are two categories of fasting: A proclaimed fast (Joel 1:14) and, a personal fast—as Jesus described in Matthew, chapter six.

First of all, I want to make this point clear. You do not fast to impress God. Some people think that if they fast long enough, it will influence Him to do something for them. To punish yourself does not impress the Lord. It will only make you very, very hungry! Fasting changes *you*, not God.

Let's look at a *proclaimed fast*. Sometimes situations arise in which you need divine direction. A proclaimed fast is for the purpose of bringing believers into a place of hearing from God. When you find out how to pray about the situation, you can then move in the same area of faith in one accord.

In 2 Chronicles 20:1-6, the Word says, *It came to pass after this also, that the children of Moab, and the children of Ammon, and with them other beside the Ammonites, came against Jehoshaphat to battle. Then there came some that told Jehoshaphat, saying, There cometh a great multitude against thee from beyond the sea on this side Syria; and, behold, they be in Hazazontamar, which is Engedi. And Jehoshaphat feared, and set himself to seek the Lord, and proclaimed a fast throughout all Judah. ...And Jehoshaphat stood in the congregation of Judah and Jerusalem, in the house of the Lord, before the new court, And said, O Lord God of our fathers, art not thou God in heaven...and in thine hand is there not power and might, so that none is able to withstand thee?*

The main reason that a proclaimed fast brings results is that it causes the people's minds to go in one direction. That direction is toward God. They drop all other things and center their attention on Him. This brings His manifested presence in their midst.

While these believers were all in one accord, it says, *Then upon Jahaziel the son of Zechariah, the son of Benaiah, the son of Jeiel, the son of Mattaniah, a Levite of the sons of Asaph, came the Spirit of the Lord in the midst of the congregation.* Did you notice that the Spirit of God did not come on Jehoshaphat? He was the leader. Thank God somebody in the congregation was sensitive to the Holy Spirit. *And he said, Hearken ye, all Judah, and ye inhabitants of Jerusalem, and thou king Jehoshaphat, Thus saith the Lord unto you, Be not afraid nor dismayed by reason of this great multitude; for the battle is not yours, but God's* (2 Chron. 20:15). Imagine how good that sounded to their ears! The Holy Ghost spoke. That is what they were seeking!

This will work in our day. Here is a New Testament example. Acts 13:1,2 says, *Now there were in the church that was at Antioch certain prophets and teachers...As they ministered to the Lord, and fasted, the Holy Ghost said, Separate me Barnabas and Saul for the work whereunto I have called them.* That assignment brought into being two thirds of the New Testament. What an important day! Those men did not realize the magnitude of God's plan. They were simply being obedient.

The Holy Ghost spoke in the midst of a group of ordinary men. They were fasting and praying and ministering unto the Lord. This set into motion something that absolutely changed the world!

In that kind of atmosphere, God is given the opportunity to speak. **A proclaimed fast is valuable and**

effective because it causes unity and singleness of purpose. It is the same principle as the prayer of agreement or united prayer. It produces power.

They received their instructions from God. They laid their hands on Saul and Barnabas and sent them forth. The results of their ministry were astounding!

In the sixth chapter of Matthew, Jesus spoke of the *personal fast*. Matthew 6:16-18: *Moreover when ye fast, be not, as the hypocrites, of a sad countenance: for they disfigure their faces, that they may appear unto men to fast. Verily I say unto you, They have their reward. But thou, when thou fastest, anoint thine head, and wash thy face; That thou appear not unto men to fast, but unto thy Father which is in secret: and thy Father, which seeth in secret, shall reward thee openly.* Jesus really put the responsibility on you and me here. He did not say, if you fast, He said when you fast.

Rewards for personal fasting are on two different levels. One is from the admiration of men. They say, "Oh, can he fast. Oh, I wish I could do that. Don't you know he's spiritual." Jesus said not to be a hypocrite and look sad, making it obvious to men that you are fasting!

An open reward comes from God when you fast in secret. You can believe for this reward when you go into the fast. Be specific about its purpose. If you believe for the reward from the onset, the pressure of your physical body will lessen. Remembering the results and the reward being obtained makes fasting easier.

Fasting in the New Testament is not for chastisement. To chastise means to instruct. *For whom the Lord loveth he chasteneth...* (Heb. 12:6). He uses His Word to teach you.

New Testament and Old Testament repentance are two different things. Old Testament repentance meant to be sorry to the point of self-infliction or mourning. Under the new covenant, the word "repentance" means "to completely turn around; to change your mind."

If you are a born-again Christian, God will not chastise you physically through punishment. He will instruct you spiritually (Heb. 12:9). Jesus said, ...*the words that I speak unto you, they are spirit, and they are life* (John 6:63). He will use His Word.

How did Peter strike the mens' hearts on the day of Pentecost? With the words he preached. They were anointed, Holy Ghost-filled words that pricked their hearts. The Bible says that the Word of God is good for reproof and correction (2 Tim. 3:16). In the literal Hebrew, Isaiah 53:5 says, "He bore our chastisement by punishment." You never ever have to be punished by God. He deals with you through His Word!

Punishment is not in God's order of things for His family. He is available to lead you and care for you. His desire is to abundantly supply your every need according to His riches in glory.

With these things in mind, I want to study the 58th chapter of Isaiah. God explains the kind of fast to which He is calling the body of Christ. He said, *Is not this the fast that I have chosen? To loose the bands of wickedness, to undo the heavy burdens, and to let the oppressed go free, and that ye break every yoke?*

We *have been* delivered from the power of darkness through the substitutionary sacrifice of Jesus. The price has been paid. If there is any oppressive yoke, the believer *can* and *should* be free of it. **This is the fast that God has chosen: to loose the bands of wickedness, to undo the heavy burdens, to let the oppressed go free and to break EVERY enslaving yoke** (Is. 58:6). You can fast to set your whole congregation free of Satan's oppression. God calls us to fast to bring the spirit man into ascendancy over the flesh. This enhances intercession and sets the captives free!

There are also personal, spiritual rewards. Verse eight of Isaiah 58 says, *Then (when you have fasted) shall thy light break forth as the morning, and thine health shall spring forth speedily....* What is the light of God? *The entrance of thy words giveth light...* (Ps. 119:130). You begin to receive things from the light of God's Word. He will reveal His Word to you. You have confidence in the Word when you have revelation knowledge of it.

God told Joshua to meditate the Word day and night and he would *observe to do* all that was written therein (Josh. 1:8). In other words, it will be revealed to you how to act on what is written in the Word.

He also said that your *health* will spring forth speedily. Many Christians are not walking in divine health because they are ruled by the flesh. Fasting causes the spirit man to dominate the flesh. Faith for healing is easy when you are walking in the spirit.

Isaiah 58 continues to say that the presence of God will be your rear guard. The armor of God described in Ephesians six is all frontal.

Conditional to this fast is that all strife, talebearing and backbiting be purged. Every form of false, unkind or unjust speaking must be put away. The believer MUST operate in the love of God. Paul said, *Though I bestow all my goods to feed the poor...and have not charity, it profiteth me nothing.*

These conditions prevent Satan from coming in and destroying the effectiveness of the fast. If you are not operating in love, your fasting will not profit you.

Fasting helps you to tune into the spirit realm where healing and all of your inheritance already belong to you. Fasting will shut down the influences of the five physical senses so that you can walk in the spirit. Your healing, your victory, your strength, your faith, the power of God are all in the spirit. You fast so that you can walk in the spirit and enjoy your inheritance.

This is what Jesus meant when the disciples came to

Him and said, "Why could we not cast that devil out?" (Mark 9:28). Jesus did not say, "Because you haven't fasted." He said, "Because of your unbelief" (Mark 9:19). He had already given them the power to cast him out (Luke 10:19). They had been letting their flesh rule them. They were not fasting and praying and meditating on what Jesus had told them.

Jesus separated Himself to pray and fast regularly. He could minister to the people in faith. He stayed tapped into His power source—the Holy Spirit. He lived in obedience to God. **A fasted life, which is fasting and praying, and spending time in the Word, and ministering to the Lord will keep you in a position to receive from God.**

Take the time to get before God. Separate yourself from the things of the world and fast. I am talking about fasting with rewards. Jesus said the Father would reward you.

Sometimes the only reward that I seek in a fast is the deliverance of a friend, a situation that needs correcting, or God's anointing to minister more effectively. I fast and *expect* the anointing of God to operate.

A man living a fasted life lays things aside just to be with God. Once I fasted my newspaper. I had been spending anywhere from 15 minutes to an hour reading it everyday. For one week I laid it aside to read the Word of God instead. Years have come and gone and I have not gone back to it. God honored that fast.

If you really want to enjoy life and break completely out of the ordinary, begin to live the high life of which Jesus spoke. He said, "If you will lose your life for My sake, you'll find it" (Matt. 10:39). The Greek text says, "If you'll give up that low life, you will find the high life." This is one of the ways you shed the low life. The high life in the realm of the spirit is *more* than exciting! It is not just a religion full of "do's" and "don'ts."

As you begin to live the fasted life, the power in the spirit will begin to work for you. You will be building your foundation on God. *A fasted life is one that feeds on the Word of God all of the time and separates itself to God. It is a life consecrated and dedicated to Him.*

Here is a six-step check list for fasting. Put yourself in a position to receive from God spiritually. You can take these steps and order your thinking by them. (1) Decide the purpose of the fast. (2) Proclaim the fast before the Lord. (3) Believe you receive the reward (Matt. 6:18) —*before* the fast. The reward will probably be related to the first step. The purpose of the fast will have a great deal to do with the rewards involved. If you are fasting for revelation knowledge, the reward would be receiving the knowledge you desire. (4) Minister to the Lord. *Let the word of Christ dwell in you richly in all wisdom; teaching and admonishing one another in psalms and hymns and spiritual songs, singing with grace in your hearts to the Lord* (Col. 3:16). These scriptures will tell you how to minister to the Lord. One of the best things you can do is to read the Psalms. You minister to the Lord by speaking of His mighty works. When you begin to praise and minister to Him, He will get involved with you! You need to fellowship with Him. He needs to hear praise and thanksgiving. I heard myself saying to the Lord one day, "Jesus, You are my High Priest. Take my praise and minister it unto my Father. Make it a sweet incense to His nostrils. Blot out all of the sin that has come up before Him from this miserable planet. Minister my praise and love and adoration to Him. Cause it to be just what He needs today. I want to bless His heart. I do not want Him to be grieved by the sinfulness of man." I began to realize that my heavenly Father needs this. Earthly fathers know what it is like for one of their children to tell them how much they love them instead of just begging for things. "I love you, Dad," is a statement that captures a father's heart. Just think how much that means to our heavenly Father. (5) Minister to others. Always minister to others *after* the fast! You need to use the spiritual power within you to meet the needs of people. If you fast according to the Word of God, you will be spiritually built up. Minister to others *during* the fast *only* as you are led of the Father to do so.

Living the fasted life will cause you to produce the fruit of the spirit according to Galatians, the fifth chapter, verse 22. These come forth from the reborn human spirit. The Holy Spirit is certainly all these things but He is not in you to bear fruit. He is in you to teach you *how* to bear fruit. He is your Teacher, your Intercessor, your Standby, your Helper. **He gives you the power—you bear the fruit.**

Galatians 5:22,23 says, *But the fruit of the Spirit is love, joy, peace, longsuffering (patience), gentleness, goodness, faith, Meekness, temperance: against such there is no law.* These are spiritual forces. Proverbs 4:20-23 says, *My son, attend to my words; incline thine ear unto my sayings. Let them not depart from thine eyes; keep them in the midst of thine heart. For they are life unto those that find them, and health to all their flesh. Keep thy heart with all diligence; for out of it are the issues of life.* One translation says, *Out of it (the heart) flow the forces of life.* Not one single force in this list will produce death. Love produces life. Joy is a life-giving force, etc.

Fasting shuts down the influence of the body, so that the spirit man can dominate. As you stay in the Word and in fellowship with God, you will not be flesh-ruled. You will glorify God in your body.

Chapter VIII
Hindrances to Prayer

God's desire is to answer every prayer. He has even given us His Word so that we can pray according to His will. Unanswered prayer is not the result of God's unwillingness to use His power, but because of hindrances we allow to overcome us. The Bible says that His eyes look to and fro throughout the earth to show Himself strong in behalf of those whose hearts are perfect toward Him (2 Chron. 16:9). When we are aware of these hindrances, and how to avoid them, we will experience the joy of answered prayer.

Jesus said in Matthew 21:22, **"And all things, whatsoever ye shall ask in prayer, believing, you shall receive."** He did not say that a few things that you pray for would come to pass or that just a prayer now and then would be answered. Jesus said, "And *all* things, whatsoever ye shall ask in prayer believing." He said *believing*. Then "you shall receive."

Doubt and Unbelief

Two of the greatest hindrances to the believer's prayer life are doubt and unbelief. Although they are similar, they are two different things. **Doubt is the thief of God's greater blessings.** It keeps a man in a state of separation from Him. Some men doubt that there is a God. They doubt that He will perform His Word in response to their prayers. As a result they do not respond to God's Word. This hinders His power in their behalf.

Doubt comes from ignorance of God's Word. For example, so many people have the idea that God will no longer heal. They think that He is not interested in their financial affairs. Consequently, their prayers will be hindered.

God has given us a way to keep our minds renewed. It is through the knowledge of His Word. We can fellowship with Him, find out His attitude, and act accordingly. For instance, a man determines that it is God's will to heal him. When he prays according to God's Word, he can be sure God will move in his behalf, thus expelling the force of doubt.

Unbelief is when a man knows there is a God, yet does not believe His Word. He knows what the Bible says, but he has chosen to believe what he can see and feel instead. This will definitely hinder his prayer life.

In order to expel doubt and unbelief, you must make God's Word final authority in every matter. Do not allow what religious tradition says or what *you* think about it to be the deciding factor. Pray according to the will of God and believe you receive when you pray. God's Word is His will. He does not will one thing and say something else. God cannot lie. Refuse to be moved by anything except what God's Word tells you.

When you pray, expect things to change. God's Word will not fail.

Lack of Knowledge of Our Right-standing with God

The second great hindrance to prayer is the lack of knowledge of our right-standing with God. Most people do not understand what God has actually done in Christ Jesus at Calvary. Jesus became our sin so we could become the righteousness of God (2 Cor. 5:21). Righteousness is right-standing with God. Your righteousness is vitally important in the field of prayer. We saw in the sixth chapter of Ephesians that righteousness is a breastplate.

Your right-standing with God gives you the right to approach God in prayer without a sense of guilt, sin, or condemnation. There is a confidence you experience knowing that you will receive when you ask in faith believing.

Every man, whether he is a sinner or part of the family of God, has a God-given right to pray and expect results. Romans 3:21-23 says, *But now the righteousness of God without the law is manifested, being witnessed by the law and the prophets; Even the righteousness of God which is by faith of Jesus Christ unto all and upon all them that believe: for there is no difference: For all have sinned, and come short of the glory of God.* The Apostle Paul said that the right to expect God to answer your prayers is upon *all* and unto *all* them that believe. No man on earth deserves God's righteousness. But when he receives Jesus as Lord, he is placed in right-standing with God. He is *made* the righteousness of God by *grace* through *faith.*

The Word says that God is not holding sin against the world (2 Cor. 5:17-21). He sent Jesus to take your place. If you recognize this and let Him be your righteousness, God will answer your prayer as if Jesus Himself prayed it. When you realize that, you have your breastplate of righteousness working for you. You have something priceless working in your life.

You may think you are the worst sinner the world has ever seen. Any man who considers himself so far gone that God cannot reach him, must think that he is bigger than God. Through the new birth Jesus has made us the righteousness of God through Calvary. No sin that Satan could dream up is big enough to change that!

Romans 5:17 says, *For if by one man's offense death reigned by one.* That, of course, was the offense committed by Adam in the Garden of Eden. It brought death into the earth. *Much more they which receive abundance of grace and of the gift of righteousness shall reign in life by one, Jesus Christ.* As born-again believers, we have been made the righteousness of God in Christ. Therefore, we have been given the ability to reign in this life. We must take advantage of our right-standing relationship with God. It is then that we will see the results we desire in prayer.

James 5:16 says, *The effectual fervent prayer of a righteous man availeth much.* You may have read that verse of scripture and thought, "You know, if I were just righteous..." **Jesus died for you!** The righteousness He bought for you at Calvary is more than enough to make your prayers effective.

God is moved when a man believes His Word. Romans 5:17 says that righteousness is a gift. Romans 3:21-23 says that, *It is unto all of them that believe.* If you are believing, then, James 5:16 is true when it says that your prayer will avail much. Faith qualifies you for answered prayer!

You have a God-given right to expect God to answer your prayer. Don't let the devil deceive you into thinking that God will not answer. Jesus said that whatsoever you shall ask the Father in His name, He will give it to you. As long as you can pray believing, you will not be defeated. If you know your right-standing with God, you will not be overcome.

Ignorance of Our Right to Use the Name of Jesus

Lack of knowledge of our right to use the name of Jesus is the third great hindrance to prayer. A great void of knowledge of the power in Jesus' name exists in most Christian circles. John 16:23 says, *And in that day ye shall ask me nothing. Verily, verily, I say unto you, Whatsoever ye shall ask the Father in my name, he will give it to you.*

Go before the Father in Jesus' name. You are going before God in Jesus' power, in His faith. As a result, your prayer will be answered.

No believer would ever doubt the power of Jesus' name or that the Father hears that name in prayer. What, then, is the problem? Where is the unbelief where the name of Jesus is concerned? The root of it is in believing we have the right to use that name. Will the Father hear *me* pray in that name?

I have a right to use my name because it was given to me by my father. He was the one who sired me. He gave me the name of Kenneth Copeland. I came into the world with the right to use it. When you make Jesus Christ the Lord of your life, God becomes your Father. The Bible says that any man that believes that Jesus is the Christ is born of God (1 John 5:1). Once you realize that you have the right to use the family name, you will see God's power operating mightily in your behalf.

Gloria and I were driving down the freeway one day. The car in front of us began to fishtail. The second time it came across the freeway, it hit the curb and started up on its side. Gloria shouted at the top of her voice, "Jesus, help them." It was so strong when she shouted the name of Jesus that the car slammed back down on all four wheels and straightened out, coming to a full stop. God hearkens to that name!

I believe Satan and his cohorts are reminded of their defeat at Calvary everytime they hear the name of Jesus!

You should become so aware of the power in that name that you guard it like your own—because it is yours!

Unforgiveness and Strife

Another hindrance to prayer is found in verse 25 of Mark the 11th chapter. It says, *And when ye stand praying, forgive, if ye have ought against any: that your*

Father also which is in heaven may forgive you your trespasses. But if ye do not forgive, neither will your Father which is in heaven forgive your trespasses. This is vital. Prayer will not work without forgiveness. I cannot overemphasize its importance. Jesus prayed, *Our Father which art in heaven, Hallowed be Thy name. Thy kingdom come, Thy will be done in earth, as it is in heaven. Give us this day our daily bread, and forgive us our trespasses as we forgive those who trespass against us.* Spiritual principles are involved here. You can keep these hindrances from stopping the results of your prayers. **Harmony makes the prayer system work.**

This attitude of forgiveness begins at home. Jesus said if any two of you will *agree* on earth, He would be in your midst. A man and his wife should be the strongest agreement force there is. Satan goes to great lengths in separating a man from his wife and family. He wants them out of agreement.

First Peter 3:7 says, *Likewise, ye husbands, dwell with them (your wives) according to knowledge (according to the Word of God), giving honour unto the wife, as unto the weaker vessel, and as being heirs together of the grace of life; that your prayers be not hindered.* If a husband is not honoring his wife as he should, his prayers are hindered. The burden of harmony is not on the wife. The husband is the authority in his household. **The power of God is available to the man and the wife who purpose to stay in harmony.**

As you come against unforgiveness and reach for harmony, you will experience Jesus in your midst! He said, *If a man love me, he will keep my words: and my Father will love him, and we will come unto him, and make our abode with him* (John 14:23).

You cannot say that you please God *and* hold something against someone. This includes your family members as well. *If a man say, I love God, and hateth his brother, he is a liar: for he that loveth not his brother whom he hath seen, how can he love God whom he hath not seen?* (1 John 4:20).

Both strife and unforgiveness hinder your prayer life. *Strife is merely acting upon unforgiveness.* James 3:16 says, *For where envying and strife is, there is confusion and every evil work.* When you take confusion and add it to Satan's work, problems arise. You will have a disaster in the making. Jesus is not in the midst of that. Determine that you are not going to respond in strife. The next time someone says something rude or unmannerly to you or about someone else, make the decision not to join in. Don't carry strife any further.

Second Timothy chapter two says that because of strife Satan can capture Christians at his will (2 Tim. 2:26). The believer belongs to God and has every right to walk free. Jesus said that the thief comes to kill, to steal, and to destroy (John 10:10). That is the only reason he gets involved in your life. **The nearest avenue to completion—being whole in spirit, soul, body, financially, and socially—is the road to peace and harmony.**

The absence of strife is the key to getting rid of confusion and evil. It is the predominate, primary prerequisite for answered prayer. Stop Satan from working in your life. You do not want him in your home or your prayer life. The first thing to do is begin to forgive. Get strife out of your life. Jesus said to ask and you will receive that your joy may be made full. Your joy will be strong.

Matthew 18:19,20 will not work just because two people *say* the same thing. The prayer of agreement that makes it work is effective because of its motivating force—*love!*

As you read this, take the opportunity right now to rid yourself of strife, disharmony or unforgiveness. You confess it. Jesus is faithful to forgive you (1 John 1:9). **Give God the opportunity to create a system of harmony around you and your prayer life will begin to work.**

Lack of Knowledge of Fellowship

Lack of knowledge of the value of fellowship with God will hinder your prayer life. If you do not know the importance of a close, intimate fellowship with God, you will not likely see results in prayer. Set apart a specific time to be alone with Him. Direct all of your attention toward Him. It is easy to say, ''I don't have time to stop everything else, so I'll just fellowship with God 'on the go.' If He has something to tell me, He can say it while I'm doing this or that.'' You can commune with God wherever you are and whatever you are doing. However, you must get quiet and spend quality time in His presence to hear His voice. When you are ''on the go,'' *you* will do most of the talking.

The Bible says in 1 John 1:3,4, *That which we have seen and heard declare we unto you, that ye also may have fellowship with us: and truly our fellowship is with the Father, and with his Son Jesus Christ. And these things write we unto you, that your joy may be full.* You are called into fellowship with the Father. Why do you suppose God made a man in the first place? He created man for fellowship. You were created for *His* pleasure.

The Bible says that we have been given in our spirit a cry that says, ''Abba, Father.'' Greek scholars tell us that the closest English word we have to ''abba,'' is ''daddy.'' Our relationship with Him has all of the freedom of ''Daddy,'' and yet the reverence and respect of our ''Father.'' You can fellowship with God on both levels, as your Daddy and as your Father.

Fellowshipping with the Father gives Him the opportunity to reveal His Word to you by His Spirit. Fellowship brings joy to your relationship. Jesus said, *Your joy no man can take from you!* That joy is your strength.

The Word of God brings faith. Fellowship will cause it to become effective. Fellowship will drive out all fear and doubt. It brings you into a love relationship with the Father. Love casts out fear. Through intimate fellowship, God will personally reveal His love to you.

You fellowship with the Father because you desire His company and not out of a lack of faith. Do it because you love God and He loves you. Take it for granted that this is the way it is going to be. Your relationship is founded on love instead of obligation when you *choose* to fellowship with God.

God and His Word are one. You fellowship with Him through His Word. Then He responds to you by His Spirit. Learn to fellowship with God. Do it by faith and expect Him to respond. Say, "Father, I didn't come to beg You for *things.* I came to visit with You. You have things to tell me and I'm going to be quiet and just listen. I want to hear from You. Most of all, I just want to be with You in Your presence. I want to watch You run the universe. I want Your slightest whim to be my command."

The first time I did that, the Lord spoke to me and said, "Son, you don't know how that thrills the heart of a Father." I heard Him speak to me in words you hear when you talk with a friend. I heard it in my heart as if it were an audible voice. Psalm 16:11 says that fullness of joy is in His presence. What joy it brought.

He enjoys our fellowship, too. It brings Him fulfillment and joy as well. **The greatest times you will ever have are times spent fellowshipping with God!**

Chapter IX
A Deeper Life in Prayer

To summarize, I want to share some necessary guidelines in the development of a deeper life in prayer. These will cause your prayer life to become accurate.

Scriptural principles of prayer will bring about an accurate prayer life. *Accuracy produces results.* When you get accurate in your prayer life things will happen. Charles Finney wrote in one of his memorandums, "I have had some experiences in prayer of late that have alarmed me." I thought about that for a while. I realized I hadn't really had any prayer experiences that were "alarming." I made the decision to get involved in my prayer life like he did. As my prayer life deepened, I began to have some awesome experiences.

When you are accurate in your prayer life, you are operating out of your spirit man rather than just out of your mind. Your spiritual ears are open to the voice of God. Train yourself not to make a move without listening to the Spirit of God. He is the Intercessor. You are the mouthpiece. *Likewise the Spirit also helpeth our infirmities: for we know not what we should pray for as we ought: but the Spirit itself maketh intercession for us with groanings which cannot be uttered* (Rom. 8:26). If you never attempt to be accurate in prayer, you will never be sure about the results. You'll just be hoping for something to happen.

The Holy Spirit coming to us changed the whole perspective of prayer. This is a key to accuracy. Jesus said, *And in that day* (after the Holy Spirit comes) *ye shall ask me nothing. Verily, verily, I say unto you, Whatsoever ye shall ask the Father in my name, he will give it you. Hitherto have ye asked nothing in my name: ask, and ye shall receive, that your joy may be full. These things have I spoken unto you in proverbs: but the time cometh, when I shall no more speak unto you in proverbs, but I shall shew you plainly of the Father. At that day ye shall ask in my name: and I say not unto you, that I will pray the Father for you: For the Father himself loveth you, because ye have loved me, and have believed that I came out from God* (John 16:23-27).

Pray to the Father in Jesus' name. Jesus is the Endorser of your prayer. With His name you are given free access to the throne of God. You cross-circuit the system when you make your requests to Jesus. He said, "Pray this way—Our Father, which art in heaven, hallowed be thy name" (Luke 11:2). If you want Jesus endorsing your prayer then you need to pray to the Father in His name.

Believe that you receive when you pray. Mark 11:24 states, *Therefore I say unto you, What things soever ye desire, when ye pray, believe that ye receive them, and ye shall have them.* The *Amplified Bible* says, *For this reason I am telling you, whatever you ask for in prayer, believe—trust and be confident—that it is granted to you, and you will [get it].* Make note of the word "granted." John 16:23 in the *Amplified* says, *And when that time comes, you will ask nothing of Me—you will need to ask Me no questions. I assure you, most solemnly I tell you, that My Father will grant you whatever you ask in My name.* To grant means "to bestow possession of by title of deed." You need no other evidence than God's Word. **Believe that you receive.** Learn to do this *everytime* you pray. Learn to pray with your Bible open. Do not major on the problem. Start with the answer. Be specific when you pray. God said He would watch over His Word to perform it (Jer. 1:12). Once you are involved in His Word, He can work for you. Be fully persuaded that God can perform His Word for you (Rom. 4:21).

Forgive. Your faith will not work accurately in an unforgiving heart. Jesus commanded us to forgive (Mark 11:24,25). Your prayers will not work effectively with sin in your life. The promises don't work without meeting the conditions.

All you have to do is confess unforgiveness. He is faithful and just to forgive you and cleanse you from all unrighteousness. Keep your prayer life exact by keeping sin out of your life. Keep the forgiveness door to your heart open. Maintain your fellowship with your Father.

Depend on the Holy Spirit in your prayer life. Romans 8:26: *Likewise the Spirit also helpeth our infirmities: for we know not what we should pray for as we ought: but the Spirit itself maketh intercession for us with groanings which cannot be uttered.* The Holy Spirit is your Helper, Standby, Teacher, Strengthener, Comforter, Intercessor, Counselor. Depend on Him when you pray. Operate in faith instead of feeling.

Allow the spirit realm to become a reality in you. Purpose to see beyond the realm of your five physical senses. You *are* a spirit. You *have* a soul. You live in a body. Your body is just the earth suit for your spirit. It is not the real you.

Many people want to see visions or see an angel appear. Seeking after something you can see with your natural eye or hear with your natural ear is the lowest form of spiritual manifestation. If you are not in tune with God spiritually, you would not be able to understand a vision if you saw one. When you become spiritually in tune you do not need any confirmation from your senses. The Word is enough evidence. God will confirm His Word to you when you are in faith (Mark 16:20). Rely on the Holy Spirit.

Learn to pray, for others. First Timothy 2:1 says, *I exhort therefore, that, first of all, supplications, prayers, intercessions, and giving of thanks, be made for all men.* Train yourself to do this **first of all.** The result of praying for others is that you live a quiet and peaceable life in all godliness and honesty. Anytime the church of Jesus Christ is in turmoil, they are not praying for others.

The Apostle Paul tells us that spiritual maturity demands each believer to do his part (Eph. 4:15,16). Verse 16 says, *From whom the whole body fitly joined together and compacted by that which every joint supplieth, according to the effectual working in the measure of every part, maketh increase of the body unto the edifying of itself in love.* Each part has a contribution to make to the rest of the body. We are to supply to one another as we draw from God through our fellowship with Him.

As you get involved through intercessory prayer for the body of Christ, the whole operation will begin to be successful. When you pray and supply the things that cause the Body to be compacted together, Satan cannot tear it down. Pray the prayer of intercession. It will cause us to come together in unity.

I suggest you set up a time and a place to pray the prayer of intercession. Even if it is just for five minutes. It will grow into ten minutes, fifteen minutes, twenty minutes and so on. Your intercession has a positive effect on the lives of others.

Spend time praying in the Spirit. Jude 20 says, *But ye, beloved, building up yourselves on your most holy faith, praying in the Holy Ghost.* Take the time to pray in other tongues specifically for edification. It will keep you prepared at all times. First Corinthians 14:4 says, *He that speaketh in an unknown tongue edifieth himself.* The word "edify" translated in the Greek means the same as "charging a battery."

Praying in other tongues will keep you tuned into the Spirit. It will help you to overcome the weakness of your flesh.

God needs a church right now that is not walking after the flesh. As we walk in the spirit and sow to the spirit, we stay "charged" and ready to do battle in the spirit! *God needs each and everyone of us in this critical time.*

Take the time daily to build yourself up praying in the Holy Ghost. It will draw you into a deeper life in prayer.

Always base your prayer on the Word of God. Prayer based on the Word is based on God's will. God's Word *is* His will. James 4:3 says, *Ye ask, and receive not, because ye ask amiss.* If you pray within the confines of God's Word, you cannot ask amiss. All scripture is profitable for correction and instruction (2 Tim. 3:16). When you pray in line with God's Word, you can have the confidence that your prayers are free from error.

Conclusion

What I have shared with you are principles and precepts from God's Word that I have put to work in my personal life and ministry. Before Jesus came into my life, I was a total failure. Any of the success that I have enjoyed has been the result of a personal relationship with Jesus and a rich prayer life.

Let me lead you into the throne room of God. You can enjoy the very best that life has to offer and experience the success that God desires for you.

Heavenly Father, I approach Your throne boldly in the name of Jesus. I have seen from Your Word that You desire to be personally involved in my life. It is Your desire to answer my prayers. I believe that Jesus died and suffered the punishment for my sins so that I could experience a close relationship with You as my heavenly Father. I can see from Your Word that I have the right to expect my prayers to be answered—not based on my worthiness, but based on my right-standing in Christ Jesus. Your Word says that if I draw nigh unto You, that You will draw nigh unto me. I desire a more personal relationship with You. I want to experience a rich and successful prayer life. I thank You for the love that You have expressed toward me through Your Word. I will respond to that love right now and expect You to manifest Yourself in my life as I act on Your Word in faith. As I apply the principles that I have learned, I expect to see the results of an accurate prayer life. I thank You and praise You for Your faithfulness, in Jesus' name. Amen!

Prayers

Putting Prayer to Work!

Prayer that is based on the Word is already in line with the will of God. First John 5:14,15 tells us that we know God hears us and answers our prayer when we ask according to His will. The following prayers have been compiled from the Word of God on various subjects. They will aid you in getting your personal prayer life off to a good start.

I have included some very brief instruction for making Jesus your Lord and for receiving the Holy Spirit. Of course, there is much more; these are only to get you started. God will honor your prayers and give you direction.

Some of these prayers are confessions of the Word of God and not petitions. Psalm 103:20 says, *Bless the Lord, ye his angels, that excel in strength, that do his commandments, hearkening unto the voice of his word.* The angels hearken to God's Word and cooperate with Him in bringing it to pass in your behalf. God is alert and active, watching over His Word to perform it (Jer. 1:12). Confession of the Word, by the believer activates the power of God. He has said, *So shall My Word be that goes forth out of My mouth; it shall not return to Me void—without producing any effect, useless—but it shall accomplish that which I please and purpose, and it shall prosper in the*

93

thing for which I sent it (Is. 55:11, *Amplified Bible*). As you speak God's Word over situations and circumstances, it will produce a positive effect and prosper in those areas.

Scriptures used in the following prayers and confessions are taken from the King James Version and the Amplified Bible.

To Make Jesus the Lord of Your Life

Do you know where you stand with God?

If you have never made Jesus the Lord of your life, then you are separated from God through sin. You are the reason God sent Jesus to the cross. John 3:16 says, *For God so loved the world, that he gave his only begotten Son, that whosoever believeth in him should not perish, but have everlasting life.* God loved *you* so much that He gave His only begotten Son for *you*.

Second Corinthians 5:21 says that God made Jesus, Who knew no sin, to be sin for us. Jesus was the spotless Son of God. He knew no sin; but God made Him to be sin *for* us. **Sin was the reason Jesus came to earth. He died on the cross and went to hell for one reason: to pay the price for sin.** Once that price was paid, Jesus was raised from the dead, triumphant over Satan; and the sin problem was taken care of.

God is not holding your sin against you. He sent Jesus as your Substitute. He paid the debt, now you can receive the credit for what He did in your place (Is. 53:3-5).

The price has been paid, but it's not an automatic thing. You must *choose* to receive Jesus as your personal Savior. If you have never done so, choose Him now. Repent of your sin, turn totally from it and pray. When you do, the power of God will make you a new creature in Christ Jesus.

"Heavenly Father, in the name of Jesus, I present myself to You.

"I pray and ask Jesus to be Lord over my life. I believe it in my heart, so I say it with my mouth: Jesus has been raised from the dead. This moment, I make Him the Lord over my life.

"Jesus, come into my heart. I believe this moment that I am saved. I say it now: I am reborn. I am a Christian. I am a child of Almighty God."

Scripture References: John 1:12, 3:16, 6:37, 10:10; Romans 3:23; 2 Corinthians 5:17,19,21; John 16:8,9; Romans 5:8; John 14:6; Romans 10:9,10,13.

To Be Filled with the Holy Spirit

Jesus Christ, after He was raised from the dead and before He ascended into heaven, left us this promise. "Ye shall receive power, after that the Holy Ghost is come upon you: and ye shall be witnesses unto me throughout the earth" (Acts 1:8). The Holy Spirit is the One Who endues us with power for our Christian walk and to do the works of Jesus (John 14:12).

God has already sent the Holy Spirit. He came to earth on the day of Pentecost (Acts, chapter two). Now it is up to you to receive Him into your life.

Once you are born again, you can receive the Holy Spirit just as you received Jesus—by faith in God's Word. All you must do is ask Him. Jesus said, *If ye then being evil, know how to give good gifts unto your children: HOW MUCH MORE shall your heavenly Father give the Holy Spirit to them that ask him?* (Luke 11:13). The Holy Spirit will empower you with God's own power! You need His power working in you, ask Him now.

"My heavenly Father, I am a believer. I am Your child and You are my Father. Jesus is my Lord. I believe with all my heart that Your Word is true.

"Your Word says that, if I will ask, I will receive the Holy Spirit, so in the name of Jesus Christ, my Lord, I am asking You to fill me to overflowing with Your precious Holy Spirit. Jesus, baptize me in the Holy Spirit.

"Because of Your Word, I believe that I now receive and I thank You for it. I believe that the Holy Spirit is within me and, by faith, I accept it.

"Now, Holy Spirit, rise up within me as I praise my God. I fully expect to speak with other tongues, as You give me the utterance."

Meditate these scriptures on the Holy Spirit: Luke 11:9-13; John 14:10,12,16,17; Acts 1:8, 2:4,32,33,39, 8:12-17, 10:44-46, 19:2,5,6; 1 Corinthians 14:2-15,18,27; Ephesians 6:18; Jude 20.

A Prayer for Salvation in Behalf of Others

"Father, I come before You in prayer and in faith, believing. Your Word says that You desire all men to be saved and come into the knowledge of the truth, so I bring (name) before You this day.

"I break the power of Satan from his assignments and activities in _____'s life in the name of Jesus. Now, while Satan is bound, I ask that You send forth the perfect laborers to share the Good News of the Gospel in such a way that he (she) will listen and understand it. As the truth is ministered, I believe _____ will come to his (her) senses and come out of the snare of the devil and make Jesus the Lord of his (her) life.

"Father, I ask that You fill _____ with the knowledge of Your will in all wisdom and spiritual understanding. As I intercede in his (her) behalf, I believe that the power of the Holy Spirit is activated and from this moment on, I shall praise and thank You for _____'s salvation. I am confident that You are alert and active, watching over Your Word to perform it. It will not return to You void. It will accomplish that which You please and prosper in the thing whereto it was sent.

"Therefore, my confession of faith is, 'God has begun a good work in _____'s life and He will perform it and bring it to full completion until the day of Jesus Christ, in Jesus' name."

Scripture References from Amplified Bible: 2 Peter 3:9; Matthew 18:18, 9:37,38; 2 Timothy 2:26; Jeremiah 1:12; Isaiah 55:11; Philippians 1:6.

A Prayer for Health and Healing

"Father, in the name of Jesus, I confess Your Word concerning healing. As I do this, I believe and say that Your Word will not return to You void, but will accomplish what it says it will. Therefore, I believe in the name of Jesus that I am healed according to 1 Peter 2:24. It is written in Your Word that Jesus Himself took my infirmities and bore my sicknesses (Matt. 8:17). Therefore, with great boldness and confidence I say on the authority of that written Word that I am redeemed from the curse of sickness and I refuse to tolerate its symptoms.

"Satan, I speak to you in the name of Jesus and say that your principalities, powers, your master spirits who rule the present darkness, and your spiritual wickedness in heavenly places are bound from operating against me in any way. I am loosed from your assignment. I am the property of Almighty God and I give you no place in me. I dwell in the secret place of the Most High God, I abide, remain stable and fixed under the shadow of the Almighty, whose power no foe can withstand.

"Now, Father, because I reverence and worship You, I have the assurance of Your Word that the angel of the Lord encamps around about me and delivers me from every evil work. No evil shall befall me, no plague or calamity shall come near my dwelling. I confess the Word of God abides in me and delivers to me perfect soundness of mind and wholeness in body and spirit from the deepest parts of my nature in my immortal spirit even to the joints and marrow of my bones. That Word is medication and life to my flesh for the law of the Spirit of life operates in me and makes me free from the law of sin and death.

"I have on the whole armor of God and the shield of faith protects me from all the fiery darts of the wicked. Jesus is the High Priest of my confessions, and I hold fast to my confession of faith in Your Word. I stand immovable and fixed in full assurance that I have health and healing NOW in the name of Jesus.

Scripture References: Isaiah 55:11; Galatians 3:13; James 4:7; Ephesians 6:12; 2 Corinthians 10:4; Psalm 91:1, 34:7, 91:10; Proverbs 4:22; Romans 8:2; Ephesians 6:16; Hebrews 4:14; Psalm 112:7. Amplified Bible—2 -Timothy 1:7; Hebrews 4:12.

A Prayer for a Harmonious Marriage

"Father, in the name of Jesus, it is written in Your Word that love is shed abroad in our hearts by the Holy Ghost Who is given to us. Because You are in us, we acknowledge that love reigns supreme.

"We believe that love is displayed in full expression enfolding and knitting us together in truth, making us perfect for every good work to do Your will, working in us that which is well-pleasing in Your sight.

"We desire to live and conduct ourselves and our marriage honorably and becomingly. We esteem it as precious, worthy and of great price. We commit ourselves to live in mutual harmony and accord with one another, delighting in each other, being of the same mind and united in spirit.

"Father, we believe and say that we are gentle, compassionate, courteous, tender-hearted and humbleminded. We seek peace and it keeps our hearts in quietness and assurance. Because we follow after love and dwell in peace, our prayers are not hindered in any way in the name of Jesus. We are heirs together of the grace of God.

"We purpose together to live in agreement, to live in harmony, to live in peace, to live in power toward each other and toward all men. We confess that our marriage grows stronger day by day in the bond of unity because it is founded on Your Word and rooted and grounded in Your love. Father, we thank You for the performance of it in Jesus' name."

Scripture References from Amplified Bible: Romans 5:5; Philippians 1:9; Colossians 3:14, 1:10; Philippians 2:13, 2:2; Ephesians 4:32; Isaiah 32:2; Philippians 4:7; 1 Peter 3:7; Ephesians 3:17,18; Jeremiah 1:12.

A Prayer for Your Children

"Father, Your Word is true and I believe it. Therefore, in the name of Jesus, I believe in my heart and say with my mouth that the Word of God prevails over my children. Your Word says that You will pour out Your Spirit upon my offspring and Your blessing upon my descendants. I believe and say that my children are wise and that they take heed to and are the fruit of godly instruction and correction. I love my children and I will diligently discipline them early. Because of that, they give me delight and rest.

"Father, I take Your Word that says You will contend with him who contends with me and You give safety to my children and ease them day by day. I confess that You, Lord, give Your angels special charge over my children to accompany and defend and preserve them. I believe they find favor, good understanding and high esteem in Your sight, Lord, and in the sight of man.

"I confess that my children are disciples taught of the Lord and obedient to Your will. Great is their peace and undisturbed composure. I believe I receive wisdom and counsel in bringing up my children in the discipline and instruction of the Lord. And Your Word declares that when they are old they will not depart from it. So, I commit them into Your keeping and I know and have confident trust that they are watched over and blessed of the Lord all the days of their lives, in Jesus' name.''

Scripture References from Amplified Bible: Mark 11:23; Isaiah 44:3; Proverbs 13:1,24, 29:17; Isaiah 49:25; Psalm 91:12; Deuteronomy 28:13; Proverbs 3:4; Isaiah 54:13; Proverbs 2:6; Ephesians 6:4; Proverbs 22:6; Deuteronomy 28:6. Also see Psalm 127:3-5; Jeremiah 1:12; Isaiah 55:11, not included in prayer.

A Prayer for Our Government

''Father, in Jesus' name, I give thanks for our country and its government. I hold up in prayer before You the men and women in positions of authority. I pray for all people in authority over us in any way. I pray that the Spirit of the Lord rests upon them.

''I believe that skillful and godly wisdom has entered into the heart of our leaders and knowledge is pleasant to them. Discretion watches over them; understanding keeps them and delivers them from the way of evil and from evil men.

''Your Word declares that 'blessed is the nation whose God is the Lord.' I receive Your blessing and declare with my mouth that Your people dwell safely in this land and that they prosper abundantly.

''It is written in Your Word that the heart of the king is in the hand of the Lord and that You turn it whichever way You desire. I believe the heart of our leader is in Your hand and that his decisions are divinely directed of the Lord.

''I give thanks unto You that the Good News of the Gospel is published in our land. The Word of the Lord prevails and grows mightily in the hearts and lives of the people. I give thanks for this land and the leaders You have given to us, in Jesus' name.

"I proclaim that Jesus is Lord over my country."

Scripture References: 1 Timothy 2:1,2; Proverbs 2:11,12. Amplified Bible —Psalm 33:12; Proverbs 21:1. Also see 1 Timothy 2:1,2; Jeremiah 1:12, not included in prayer.

To Walk in the Perfect Peace of God

"Father, in Jesus' name, I thank You that Your peace is my covenant right in Christ Jesus. I will keep my mind fixed on You Lord and trust in You and You will keep me in perfect peace.

"I will not fret or have anxiety about anything, but in every circumstance and in everything by prayer and petition with thanksgiving, I will continue to make my wants known to You, Father. And Your peace which transcends all understanding, shall garrison and mount guard over my mind and heart in Christ Jesus. I fix my mind only on that which is worthy of reverence, honorable, just, pure, lovely, kind and gracious. If there is anything worthy of praise, I will think on and weigh and take account *only* of these things.

"I will let the peace of God rule in my heart. As I do, I believe that my calm and undisturbed heart and mind are life and health to my physical body. I humble myself under the mighty hand of God, casting all of my concerns and anxieties on Him once and for all, because I know that He cares for me affectionately.

"I thank You, Father, that You have not given me a spirit of timidity, of cowardice, of craven and cringing and fawning fear. The spirit I have of You is of power and love and of calm and well-balanced mind and discipline and self-control. You, Lord, are on my side, I will not fear. What can men do to me? You, Lord, are my light and my salvation; whom shall I fear or dread? You, Lord, are the refuge and stronghold of my life; of whom shall I be afraid? I love Your law, O Lord, nothing shall offend me or make me stumble, I walk in *great* peace in Jesus' name, Amen."

Scripture Reference: Isaiah 26:3. Amplified Bible—Philippians 4:6-8; Colossians 3:15; Proverbs 14:30; 1 Peter 5:6,7; 2 Timothy 1:7; Psalm 118:6; Psalm 119:165.

Walking in the Wisdom
and Guidance of the Holy Spirit

"Father, in the name of Jesus, I realize that as a believer, my body is the temple of the Holy Spirit. My acknowledgement of His presence on a daily basis makes my faith in Him effectual. I believe that You, heavenly Father, are leading me and guiding me by the Holy Spirit through my spirit and illuminating my mind.

As I yield to the Holy Spirit, I believe that my steps are ordered of the Lord. Committing and trusting myself wholly to His guidance, I expect Him to cause my thoughts to become agreeable to His will and so shall my plans be established and succeed. I trust in the Lord with all my heart and lean not on my own understanding. As I acknowledge Him, He directs me in paths of righteousness.

"I confess that as I become more God-inside-minded, I can more easily recognize the inward witness of the Holy Spirit. I hear the voice of the Good Shepherd and a stranger's voice, I will not follow. I am conscious of my spirit being the candle of the Lord.

"I meditate in the Word day and night, not letting it depart from my mouth. I test my inward witness with the Word, for the Spirit and the Word agree. I am quick to act on the Word, as well as the prompting of my spirit. I am not a hearer only, but a doer. Therefore, I am blessed in all my deeds."

Scripture References: 1 Thessalonians 5:23; 1 Corinthians 6:19; Philemon 6; John 16:13; Romans 8:14; Psalm 37:23; Proverbs 16:3, 3:5,6; Psalm 23:3; Romans 8:16; John 10:27; Proverbs 20:27; Romans 8:5, 8:2; Joshua 1:8; 1 John 5:7; James 1:25.

A Prayer for Your Finances

"Heavenly Father, I have chosen Jesus as the Lord of my life and I seek first the kingdom of God and His righteousness, believing that the material things that I need will be supplied. I choose for my character and moral disposition to be free from the love of money, greed, lust and craving for earthly possessions. I am satisfied with my present circumstances and with what I have, being confident because You have promised that You will not in any way fail me, nor leave me without support. I am confident in Your faithfulness, that You will never leave me, nor forsake me, nor leave me helpless. I take comfort and am encouraged; I boldly say, 'The Lord is my Helper, I will not be seized with alarm, I will not fear, or dread or be terrified.'

"I believe, Father, that You wish above all things that I prosper and be in health even as my soul prospers. I will meditate in Your Word day and night, not letting it depart from my mouth, keeping it in the midst of my heart, observing to do all that is written therein. I believe that then, I shall make my way prosperous and have good success. As a doer of the Word, You have promised that I will be blessed in all of my deeds. I am assured that You will withhold no good thing from me as I walk uprightly. The uncompromising are never forsaken. I make it my ambition to live quietly and peacefully, to mind my own affairs, to work with my hands so that I may bear myself becomingly, correctly and honorably and command the respect of the outside world being self-supporting, dependent on no one and having need of nothing.

Knowing through Your Word, Father, that You are the Lord my God Who teaches me to profit and Who leads me by the way I should go, I will put Your principles to work in my life regarding employment. I wish to apply myself to good deeds—to honest labor and honorable employment—so that I may be able to meet necessary demands whenever the occasion may require and that I may not live an idle, uncultivated unfruitful life, in Jesus' name.

"I labor so that I may walk honestly toward those who are without. As I give, it is given unto me again, good measure, pressed down, shaken together and running over, will men give into my bosom. I do not sow sparingly and grudgingly, but rather, I sow generously, blessing others. Therefore, I can expect to reap generously and with blessings."

Scripture References: Hebrews 13:5,6; Matthew 6:33; 3 John 2; Psalm 84:11; Joshua 1:8; James 1:25; Psalm 37:25; Luke 6:38; 2 Corinthians 9:6; 1 Thessalonians 4:11,12; Isaiah 48:17; Titus 3:14.

Overcoming Bad Habits

"Father, I believe that my faith becomes effectual —divinely energized—by the acknowledging of every good thing which is in me in Christ Jesus. Through my union with Christ, I am a new creature, old things are passed away and all things have become new.

"I was crucified with Christ, nevertheless I live, yet not I, but Christ lives in me. I was buried with Him in baptism, and raised together with Him by the power of the Holy Spirit so that I might habitually live and behave in newness of life. My old, unrenewed self was nailed to the cross with Him in order that my body, which is the instrument of sin, might be made ineffective and inactive for evil and that I might no longer be the slave of sin.

"Just as death no longer has power over Jesus Christ, neither does sin have dominion over me through my union with Him. I consider myself dead to sin and my relation to it broken. I am alive only to God, living in unbroken fellowship with Him, in Christ Jesus.

104

"I have been delivered from the control and dominion of darkness and transferred into the kingdom of light. I have been raised together with Christ and am seated together with Him, far above principalities, powers, rulers of the darkness of this world and wicked spirits in high places. Sin shall no longer exert dominion over me, but I have dominion over sin. It is under my feet, in the name of Jesus, Amen."

Scripture References: Philemon 6; 2 Corinthians 5:17; Galatians 2:20; Romans 6:4,6; Romans 6:10,11; Colossians 1:13; Ephesians 2:6; Ephesians 1:21; Ephesians 6:12; Romans 6:14.

Spiritual Growth

"Heavenly Father, I cease not to pray for _____, that You may grant him (her) a spirit of wisdom and revelation—of insight into mysteries and secrets—in the deep and intimate knowledge of God, by having the eyes of his (her) heart flooded with light so that he (she) can know and understand the hope to which You have called him (her). And, to know how rich Your glorious inheritance is in the saints.

"I pray that _____ walk, live and conduct himself (herself) in a manner worthy of the Lord, fully pleasing to You and desiring to please You in all things, bearing fruit in every good work and steadily growing and increasing in the knowledge of God. I pray that he (she) may be invigorated and strengthened with all power by Your Spirit to exercise every kind of endurance and patience, perseverance and forbearance with joy.

"I believe that the good work You began in _____ will continue, right up to the time of Jesus' return, perfecting it and bringing it to its full completion in him (her), in Jesus' name. Amen."

Scripture References: Ephesians 1:17-21; Colossians 1:10,11; Philippians 1:6.

World Offices
of Kenneth Copeland Ministries

ENGLAND
P.O. Box 15
Bath, BA1 1GD

PHILIPPINES
Box 2067
Manila 2800

SOUTH AFRICA
P.O. Box 50830
Randburg 2125

AUSTRALIA
Private Bag 2
Randwick, N.S.W. 2031
Sydney

CANADA
P.O. Box 58248
Vancouver, BC V6P 6K1

HONG KONG
P.O. Box 73003
Kowloon, Central Post
Office

For complete catalog of books, teaching tapes and records, write:
Kenneth Copeland Ministries
Fort Worth, Texas 76192